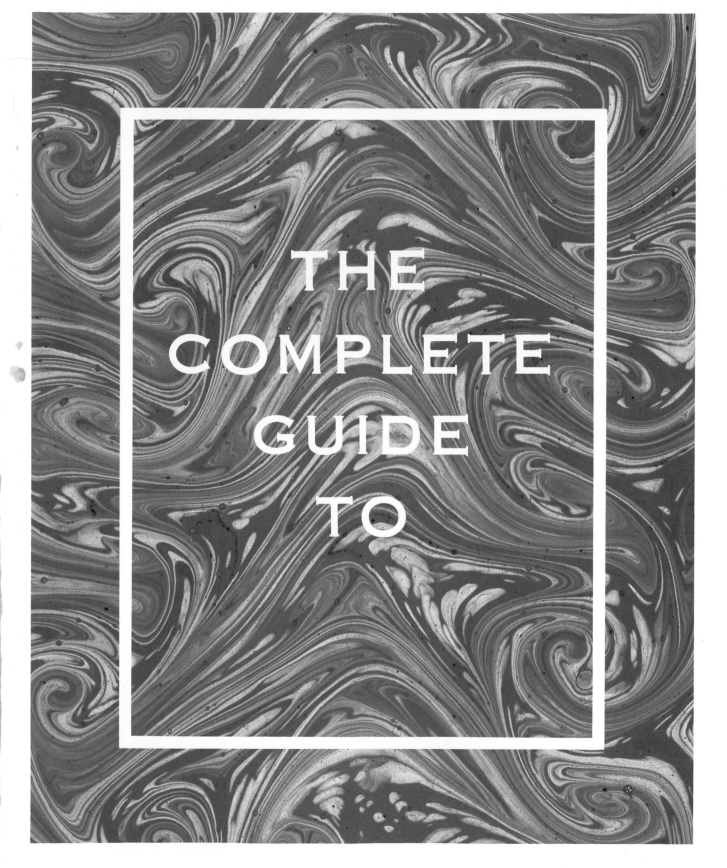

THE
COMPLETE
GUIDE
TO

Greet

DESIGN & ILLUSTRATION

BY EVA SZELA

NORTH LIGHT BOOKS

Cincinnati, Ohio

94 93 92 91   7 6 5 4

Library of Congress Cataloging-in-Publication Data

Szela, Eva, 1946—
    The complete guide to greeting card design and illustration.

    Includes index.
    1. Greeting cards. I. Title.
TT872.S94 1987   741.68'4   87-24698
ISBN 0-89134-210-9

Edited by Diana Martin
Designed by Robert Fillie

My thanks to Diana Martin for her wonderful help and support throughout this project.

CONTENTS

PERSONAL PERSPECTIVES

DEMONSTRATIONS

This is a delightful example of how a greeting card can communicate an idea or emotion without words. Since communicating feelings is such a crucial part of the successful greeting card and since not all of us can write, or have access to those who can, this is a way to create a card and not have to worry about the words. Sometimes cards without words are called "notecards," but more often they're referred to as blank cards. As a category, blank cards are en-joying more and more popularity.

INTRODUCTION

WHETHER you're just an ordinary person with no special art training, but a lot of creativity, or an artist, illustrator, or designer who's been actively practicing in your area for years, this book will help you understand all about greeting cards:

— *What they are.*

— *What they look and sound like and why.*

— *Important things to consider when creating them.*

— *Some techniques to try when doing artwork for them.*

— *Some techniques to try when writing them.*

You will learn how to create a greeting card that is just right for a specific occasion. You will see how to give that card a distinctive look that is all your own. In other words, this book will show you, no matter what your experience, how to create a greeting card that will be enjoyed, appreciated, and, if that's what you want, *very* marketable as well.

It's important to understand what a greeting card is. What exactly is it supposed to do? Think of the greeting card as a piece of stationery upon which a design as well as part or all of the letter, or "message," is already printed. The message is most important. This message is communicated through both the design *and* the words. It's the primary reason one person selects that particular greeting card to send to another person. The selection is made because whatever this particular card says coincides exactly with what the person choosing it wishes it to say. The cover might say, "This is just a small wish," and the inside could say, "for big happiness for you. Happy Birthday!" The design should augment that message. The design should help get the message across.

Another way for the message to be communicated is through the design alone. The illustration of the ecstatic cat communicates loud and clear the concept of happiness and does this completely through the design. Stop and consider for a moment how many people could send this card to someone. There are few things about it that get in the way of its broad sendability. Because of this characteristic you would say that this card is a success. Broad sendability is one of the most important signs of a successful greeting card.

Whatever the message of a particular greeting card, that message should be communicated clearly. The card must do whatever the person sending it wants it to do. If you want to cheer up an unwell friend and the card that you send cheers up your friend, then that card is a success. If you want to tell someone whom you've not seen in a long time that you are thinking about them and the card you send tells them that they are being thought about, then that card is a success. Frequently what the person sending the card wishes to communicate is both literal and emotional. "Happy Birthday!" says two things: "I remembered your birthday" and "I hope this helps you enjoy it." Sending a card that says, "Get well soon," says literally, "I want you to be physically well," and emotionally, "I hope this will cheer you up too."

The success of the greeting card means that two people are well served. The person who sends the card is satisfied that the correct message is sent and the person who receives the card understands the message and feels the appropriate, intended feeling: affection, love, cheer, laughter, any of the full gamut of human emotions or combinations of them.

These two people are the most crucial part of the entire greeting card phenomenon. This is the "sending situation." This is what the greeting card is all about, one person communicating with another through this kind of "stationery" where the letter, or "message," has been put together for her or him. Sometimes people have difficulty expressing certain kinds of feelings. They may lack confidence in their own skill with words. Greeting cards say it for them. Greeting cards, then, help people communicate. For some, who might not otherwise communicate at all, greeting cards are of extreme importance.

If you're interested in creating greeting cards that will be reproduced and marketed in large quantities, then you must consider just how broad the world of greeting cards is. The two people involved in the actual sending and receiving of the card, while important, even crucial to the success of the card, are only one of several important factors in the total success of each card. Consider two additional areas of interest: the publisher and the dealer.

THE PUBLISHER

Should you want to sell your greeting cards to someone else who will manufacture them in large quantities and distribute them, then that person becomes your immediate area of interest. The manufacturer or publisher is then your "market." This is whom you will show your artwork to. This is who will either accept it or not. That issue—the acceptance or not of *your* artwork by another party (person or corporation)—now becomes *the* issue. That acceptance or non-acceptance *now* determines the success of your greeting card. Will the manufacturer buy your greeting card and publish it? If not, then what difference does it make whether or not it succeeds at the level of the sending situation since it won't even *get* to the consumer? Now you have an additional challenge: What does the publisher look for when considering the purchase of new greeting card designs?

The publisher cares just as much as you do that the greeting card will succeed at the level of the sending situation. And so everything that's been said up to this point is now of importance to both of you. Presumably you've had an eye on the sending situation while you've been conceiving of and creating your card, and the publisher will have an eye on the sending situation while reviewing the card and considering whether or not to buy and publish it.

The publisher is thinking also about his or her most immediate market. Who does the publisher actually sell your greeting card to? Usually to each individual owner of a card and gift store or a drugstore. Sometimes to a chain of discount stores or maybe grocery stores and department stores. Everywhere that you've seen greeting cards for sale.

These places are the customers, or the "market," of the publisher. Usually the publisher sells to these outlets through sales representatives. Sales representatives are people whose job it is to act as the person going between the "account," as the customer of the publisher is sometimes called, and the publisher itself.

So the publisher will be considering, in addition to the sending situation and the likelihood that your card will fulfill one, the general impression that your card will make on the sales rep (who ought to believe in it to sell it effectively) and the owner or manager of the account, or the "dealer" (who will actually be buying it from the publisher through the sales rep). Both parties, the rep and the dealer, will probably be considering both the competition and what's sold well in the past. On the one hand they'll assess the competition: If another publisher has a product in the marketplace that is already doing the particular thing that your greeting card also does, then the market is covered, the need for it is fulfilled. Even though your version of it may be wonderful, it just isn't needed. On the other hand, they will also consider what's sold well in the past: If something in some way similar, but not too similar to your greeting card, has sold well in the past, then the likelihood of a good sales response to your card is increased, and thus the card is appealing. It's a good bet.

Additionally, all these people will be looking for something fresh and new. Because this is what the publisher's customers (sales reps and dealers) are looking for, then this is also what the publisher is looking for. You should also be considering, studying, and understanding the same things.

Consider, as well, the publisher's image. This is something that the publisher will insist on maintaining. Does your card fit in with other things this publisher sells? Is it compatible?

THE DEALER

The dealer and the dealer's perspective are important areas to consider when creating a successful greeting card. Let's say that you've got an idea for a card and it meets all the criteria of the sending situation and the requirements of the publisher. What other considerations should you make from the perspective of the dealer? The same two points that you just examined in the context of the publisher should now be reconsidered in the context of the dealer: competition and what's sold well in the past.

The dealer will be considering other issues as well: such as how much does the product cost and what kind of terms are available. But you, as the creator of the greeting card, have little influence in such areas. They are between the dealer, the sales rep, and the publisher.

WHAT SELLS, AND
WHAT DOES NOT

It's important that you know what and who your competition is. You must get to as many stores that sell greeting cards as possible. Study the areas that relate in *any* way to the kinds of greeting cards you are interested in doing. Note everything you can about these cards. Buy some and take them with you. Go back and examine them again later. Study them repeatedly. Try to benefit from their strengths and avoid what you think are their weaknesses. Your goal should be to increase your awareness, *not* copy what someone else is doing. By knowing what is out there, you can avoid duplicating looks and approaches.

The act of continuing this kind of research over a period of time has an added benefit. You will begin to acquire information about what's selling well. The successes will continue to be produced (if the publisher thinks that way—and they usually do) and the failures will disappear. So monitoring looks and concepts will begin to teach, as you continue the practice over time, what has sold and what hasn't. What sells and what does not is really the bottom line. That is what attention to the sending situation, publisher's image, competition, and what's sold well in the past—in other words, innovation based on sound thinking—is all about. Providing the consumer who walks into the dealer's store looking for the publisher's cards with the right card for her needs and wants.

It's your birthday!

We™ ©Eva Szela

Wishing you
triple dips of your favorite things
on your special day!

Happy Birthday

This Whimsical design is so lightly and delicately rendered that it is just right for a feminine Birthday card.

1 CREATING CARDS FOR EVERYDAY SENDING SITUATIONS

An unusual mood is created in the Sophisticated Stylized blank card by combining the sweet intimacy of the clown and the fluttery, delicate animation of the birds all around.

WHEN ONE person sends a greeting card to another, that is a social situation. Sending a greeting card is just like sending a letter, making a phone call, paying a visit. The person doing the sending has something to say. This chapter is about such things, which can vary widely. The sending situations described here are a few of the more common reasons one person sends a greeting card to another. One thing to note is that most greeting cards are purchased and sent by one woman to another.

Examples will be shown of how some of these sending situations have been handled by artists and designers. The challenge for you (and it can be the most fun part) is to think of new and exciting ways that *you* think

would effectively fulfill the same needs. The examples shown are ways by which you can come to understand more fully what each sending situation is all about, where some of its possibilities are. Having understood that, you will have exciting ideas of your own about how *you* would illustrate or design for that particular situation. I strongly urge you to make notes about these ideas as you go. Sometimes the ones you're certain you'll never forget can be quickly dislodged by an even more exciting one that comes to you ten seconds later.

Only everyday sending situations are examined in this chapter. Seasonal situations are examined in Chapter 4.

FRIENDSHIP

Friendship is one of the two broadest situations and is the least restrictive of them all. It's very important because it's likely to be so popular. Friendship is that situation where one person wants to send a card to another for no particular reason. It's just that she's been thinking about her friend and wants to let her know. One of the most common kinds of Friendship cards is: "Thinking of You." Most of the reasons for card sending that fall into this category are just common reasons for wanting to keep in touch with a friend or possibly someone even a little more distant emotionally than a friend. There's another one: "Keep in Touch." The illustration of the rocking chair, is an example of a greeting card that happens to fulfill both needs.

By way of further understanding this category, consider for a moment what friendship *is* to many people. Probably it's a relationship of support in a sense other than Romantic Love. Probably the friends have helped one another emotionally through one or more rough spots: maybe the stress or frustration of a job, the confusion or depression of dating, the hassle of children, perhaps even the burden of boredom. And so it makes sense for one friend to thank the other for this kind of support. That's just what the illustration of the woman with the teacup implies. Some sort of support or help was given (this particular example works for other kinds of help in addition to emotional). The illustration of the thank you card,

Thinking of You...

One of the more common sending situations for greeting cards is Friendship. And one of the more common Friendship sending situations is "Keep in Touch." In this situation one person is letting another know that she or he is remembered. This Blank Card uses light and homey, cozy references (the rocking chair, reading lamp, and sleeping cat) to communicate a feeling of warmth and affection.

page 8, is an example of another kind of Friendship card where one friend thanks the other for the very fact of their friendship. The broader version of Thank You is examined in greater detail later in this chapter.

Another aspect of Friendship is that we don't want to lose it once we've found it. And yet, we are all *so busy* that frequently we find time slipping away and one or the other person may feel that it's hurting the friendship because, let's say, one friend has moved away and neither has written or called the other in a while. The illustration on page 9 is an example of a card created to fill just this need.

The possibilities for creating greeting cards that are "right" for the category of Friendship are as limitless as your imagination. Just thinking about all the different things that characterize everyday life in America today generates the basis for a Friendship card, provided that the experience is shared by large numbers of people: "busyness" for example, "there's too little time in the craziness of life right now, so I'm sending this card to say hi,", stress, good news, missing you, bad news, conditions in other relationships, shared thoughts in general.

The idea of sharing is a big part of real friendships, so the idea of sharing is a big part of the Friendship category in greeting cards. Sharing a thought, idea, or concept is a big reason for card sending. Shared jokes are another very big area. The shared joke is the basis for the current popularity of the phenomenon called the "alternative card market." Chapter 5 examines this area in detail.

© Mary Engelbreit

One of the characteristics of any friendship is support in one form or another. This illustration is an excellent example of thanks given for such support. Symbols like the hearts being poured into the "Cup of Kindness" and the delicate and highly Feminine styling combine to make this Blank Card just right for Friendship.

(Left)
This Blank Card appeals to either a man or a woman. The graphics support the very strong editorial and do so beautifully. This is a good example of a general Friendship card where one friend is thanking the other for the very fact of their friendship.

(Right)
Urging a friend to write is a common greeting card sending situation. The editorial puts pressure on the recipient. The illustration is highly Feminine, attractive, and innocent. The use of a surprise element (the inside copy) is positive and funny. This is an excellent example of a Friendship greeting card.

... or I'll call collect.

BIRTHDAY

This is the second broad greeting card sending situation. Who doesn't have a birthday? We all know some-one's or several people's birthdays, and we frequently send a greeting card to commemorate the event. The illustration is a good example of a general, highly sendable Birthday card. This example clearly shows the criteria of a good Birthday card: make it happy and celebratory; where possible, use birthday symbols like cake, candles, confetti, streamers, and balloons.

The use of the birthday gift as a design motif is debatable. If one only sends a card and the person receives no gifts, will the visual representation of a gift on the card be depressing? Some say "yes," others, "no." But an instance where depicting a gift is safe is one where the card itself is *also* a gift, an example of which is in the illustration of the tigers, shown oppo-site. Cards especially for children enjoy some popularity within the Birthday sending situation and deserve your attention. Juvenile as a separate category is examined later in this chapter.

Other topics and subjects are also completely appropriate for this send-ing situation. It's perfectly accept-able for example, to do a beautiful floral design and simply add the words "Happy Birthday." Landscapes, animals, in fact, any subject done in any style that innately appeals to the individual for whom the card is intended can be entirely appropriate by the simple addition of these words or words to the same effect. Words alone are also a good idea, as long as they are styled in an interesting, beautiful, or handsome manner. See Chapter 8 for more on designing with lettering.

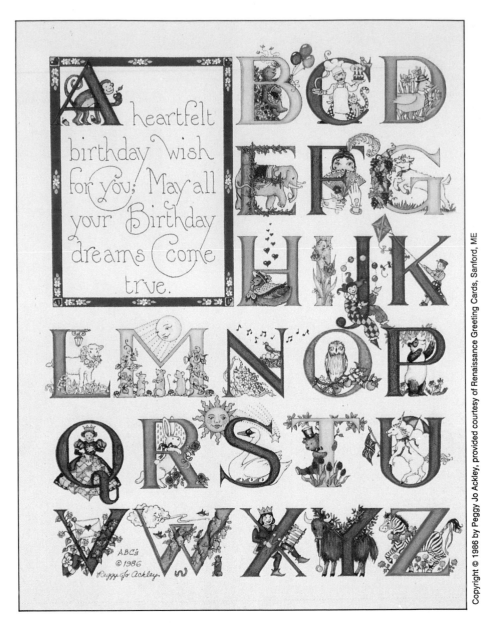

This illustration is an interesting example of the celebratory feeling and how it can work well in the Birthday sending situation. The tiny touches, balloons, teddy bears, and singing birds, are bound to make the person who receives this card feel good about having a birthday.

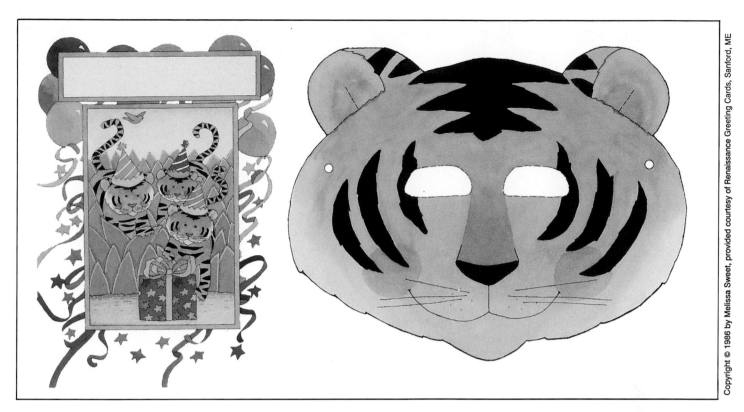

The card is designed in such a way that it is a gift (or contains a gift) and an interesting and valuable approach since its worth or apparent value is naturally increased. This card is reproduced as a three-panel unfolder. The first panel is the front of the card and the inside two panels are a tiger mask that the child can cut out and play with. This is an ingenious way to appeal to children with a greeting card.

11

" I was born October 18, 1955, and I grew up in a small, agriculturally oriented town in the Sacramento Valley of Northern California and attended public schools there. I have *always* drawn! My mother used to buy rolls of plain white shelf paper, give me a box of crayons, and I would fill the whole roll with pictures. I also loved coloring books and all kinds of crafty-stuff as a child. I won my first art award (Best in Show under Ten Years) at the county fair at age five. And I won again at age 17 in the under-eighteen category. So artwork has been a part of my life for a long, long time.

I focused on fine arts in high school and had some wonderfully encouraging teachers who spurred me on. After high school I attended the University of California, Davis, and studied there under some very well-respected artists and teachers: Wayne Thiebaud, William Wiley, and Roland Peterson. In my junior year I took a break from studio art and spent a year at New York University studying primarily art history and literature. I also discovered life in the big city! After graduating from UC Davis I moved back to New York.

I worked at different jobs (law office receptionist, patent illustrator) until a good friend encouraged me to make up a portfolio of greeting cards and take it to the New York Stationery Show. I sold two designs on the spot and that was all the encouragement I needed! After about two years of drawing cards in all my spare time and cutting back on my regular job hours, I was offered a full-time, art-oriented job if I would move to the Chicago area. Eager to do this and ready for a change, I moved to the Midwest in 1980.

I lived and worked there for almost two years. During this time I also did trade show duty and one of my locations was San Francisco (about 80 miles from where I had grown up). On one of these business trips I met my future husband, and after an 8-month long-distance romance I decided I'd had enough of the harsh Chicago winters and moved to San Francisco.

I was very lucky to be able to take my job with me. I began doing illustrations solely, sending them back to Chicago and discussing projects and changes over the phone. I still work out of my home as I have for over five years now. In June 1985 I switched to another greeting card company exclusively. Designing greeting cards is a great job and after eight years, I still love it!

I've learned several things since I began. I learned them the hard way.

• Be sure to work for an honest, reputable company.

• Get it in writing!

• Get your originals back and get the copyright under your own name (it *can* be done).

• Get an advance against royalties so you are covered financially if your design is either a slow seller or a real winner.

Some thoughts about the designs:

• For the *most* part, don't think in terms of doing a series (a fatal mistake those with a fine arts background often make). Each card must hold its own in the rack and not need a group of other cards to make it appealing.

• Greetings *are* important and can make or break a card. People prefer greetings to blank cards, since most aren't exactly sure what they want to write in a blank card.

• Concentrate on the top third of the card; that's what will be seen by the consumer in the rack. Especially if the card is written to be sent to a relative, it's *vital* to have that element in the top third.

• Work in a vertical format if it's at all possible.

• Again, think of how the card is going to be displayed.

When I'm doing my artwork I think in terms of *who* is going to buy this card: male, female, adult, child, and for what occasion. Then I try to make the appeal as broad as possible. I make each card *inviting*; it should hold something so the buyer will give it closer scrutiny. This makes the art special to me as the illustrator, and consequently it's more fun to work on.

I think a greeting card is a success if it prompts the purchaser to *pick it up* out of that sea of cards on a rack and look at it more closely. If my designs get repeat sales they're definitely a success. That kind of success is achieved by a fortuitous combination of art and greeting: art being (to *me*) the more important of the two, but greetings good or bad can most definitely decide a sale.

The successful card has a broad base of appeal and hits home somewhere with people, be it the subject matter, style, humor, thought. There are many ways to achieve that. When mine are successful I believe it's because of my great experience. After lots of trial and error I've developed a style and feeling that people relate to. Again, it's the detail, plus a sense of color and a sense of what can be *charming* and *sweet* without crossing the border of being sickeningly saccharine.

I come up with my designs in different ways. I work with the basic requirements of an occasion (for example, Valentine's Day is pink, red, and hearts). You can focus on a color, theme, or style. This is complex. I do use source material—old children's books (my current passion), art books, museum shows, magazines: trade, home, fashions, food, and so on. Inspiration comes from *many* sources and have very varied results.

I think it's important to experiment with styles *and* materials. I do many different types of card art and have discovered new methods of doing things by experimentation. And besides, if I didn't I'd be just plain *bored*. The flip side is that it will probably take me a lot longer to get recognized than it would someone whose style is distinctive and continuous.

I do some of my own writing, perhaps 25 to 30 percent of the time. I began to do it simply because it was a facet of the cards that I was involved in. I enjoyed making a greeting up to match the art. Working with different people, I now find they are extremely serious about the writing and I have to come up with a real zinger before they'll use it (even then they eventually alter a few words or a line). For me it's harder than doing artwork simply because my strength lies in *visual* rather than verbal terms.

One of the things that attracts me to greeting cards is their *size*. They are to me (at least the very best ones) like little jewels. Small pieces of wonderment that invite you to step inside the world they've created. And being small, *and* relatively affordable, you can buy this piece of art and *keep* it to treasure.

Even when I'm doing art, I enjoy the smallness of it and I do almost all my work to size. I enjoy details (perhaps compulsively so) and patterns. You'll find them in a lot of my work. I like the fact that most of it is upbeat subject matter. I like the fact that it's printed because: (1) You get to see the results fast, and being a paper product, lots of pieces come out quickly; and (2) you can send your art to all your friends and relatives! **"**

Peggy Jo Ackley's traditional Santa is benevolent, jolly, and endearing as he's Whimsically portrayed here. Santa's sack is full of strong Christmas elements like candy canes, toys, musical intruments, and a teddy bear! There are lots of red and green, and the editorial is just right for this tradition-steeped approach.

There was an old man, ever jolly and bright,
Who would make simple toys in his workshop at night.
With the hands of a craftsman and heart of a saint
He would whittle and chisel and hammer and paint.

On the night before Christmas, he'd load up his sack
And go out with his bundle of joy on his back.
He would walk 'til he'd visited each girl and boy.
They would give him a smile, he would give them a toy.

Many years have gone by since St. Nick walked the earth
Spreading joy and good tidings and magic and mirth,
Yet his spirit lives on every new Christmas eve
In the minds of the children who wait...and believe!

*Wishing you and yours
a Merry Christmas
and a Happy New Year.*

Peggy Jo Ackley ©1984

In the field of commercial greeting cards, Religious cards as a category have recently experienced tremendous growth. People of all ages and both sexes like to send Religious greeting cards. Designing Religious cards can mean a strict adherence to subject matter that is pertinent to the faith your card is intended to appeal to: Protestant, Catholic, Jewish. It can also mean that the most religious aspect of your card is the editorial and that the subject matter portrayed can be almost anything positive and upbeat. Both approaches are common. In the illustration with the heart-shaped raindrops, the words are the more predominant aspect of the card.

When the subject matter is more tra-ditionally Religious in feeling, light can play a key role in the illustration because of its highly emotional qual-ity. The illustration shown opposite, is an example of a formal, quiet way of communicating these feelings.

Feelings are really what *all* greeting cards are about. The sending situa-tion affects *which* feeling you are try-ing to bring to the recipient of the card. Almost any subject matter (flowers, people, landscapes) will work for Religious cards of a more general nature as long as the words are appropriate.

MAY LIFE SHOWER YOU WITH LOTS OF THAT LOVE FROM ABOVE

HAVE A LOVE-LY LIFE

This is an example of a Religious card that uses a general design to support an editorial beautiful-ly rendered with fine calligraphy. Hearts add to the emotional impact of this selection.

When we're feeling alone
  there is always a friend
Who is willing to share,
  to protect and defend,
Who will stand by our side,
  see us through to the end —
  Our Father.
  Our very best Friend.

This is a good example of combining an element with emotional impact and a more general illustration style to create a look with a very broad appeal that is still highly appropriate to the Religious Friendship sending situation.

LOVE NEVER FAILETH . . .

I CORINTHIANS 13:3

GOD WON'T EVER GIVE UP ON YOU.

Created by Eva Szela *Blessed Assurances*™ © Eva Szela

INSPIRATIONAL

This sending situation is very similar to the Religious one. The difference between the two is that when creating an Inspirational card you would never make a specific Religious reference either through the use of words (God, bless, holy, for instance) or through any visual key. Inspiration is a serious category. The person who sends this sort of card often wants to share an uplifting or lofty concept (sometimes, but not always, expressed through words) with the person who will receive the card. The concept, while noble, will also usually be emotional, so the use of light is a very effective tool in this category. But light is always an effective tool when you are trying to evoke a mood. The illustration with the rainbow, is a good example of an Inspirational greeting card.

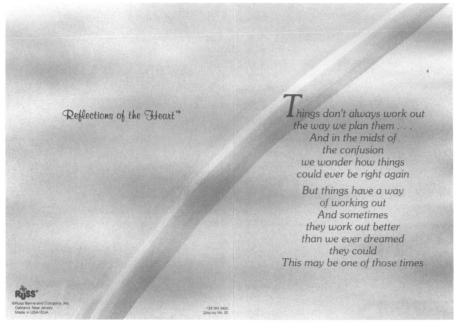

Reflections of the Heart™

*T*hings don't always work out
the way we plan them . . .
And in the midst of
the confusion
we wonder how things
could ever be right again

But things have a way
of working out
And sometimes
they work out better
than we ever dreamed
they could
This may be one of those times

This design is a beautiful example of a general Inspirational illustration. It contains effective use of light. The rainbow is always a good image to use to suggest hope or any kind of positive, uplifting feeling.

ROMANTIC LOVE

Some of those who work with greeting cards a lot see this category as part of Friendship. Perhaps there is somewhat of a relationship of friends between lovers. When someone wants to send a card to the person with whom they are in love, however, the card should be very specific about it. And because of that it will only be right for Romantic Love. It will have an image of two people interacting romantically, or it will depict two animals interacting in a romantic way. The card could also be decorated with hearts or perhaps a single, red rose. Any of these images will be just right for the sending situation. The words on the card will say something like "I love you" and will further influence the positioning of your greeting card in Romantic Love. Any of these single elements will make the card entirely inappropriate for Friendship.

Focus always on what limitations you are placing on the sendability of your card. Adding a Romantic Love element inadvertently to a Friendship card will abruptly limit the number of people to whom that card can be sent since Romantic Love is a narrower category. The *average* person has only one lover. The average person has more friends than lovers and thus more opportunity and occasion to send Friendship cards than Romantic Love cards. Understanding that is by no means a denigration of the Romantic Love sending situation as a whole. When that is what you want to create, it's important to know how to do it, and do it effectively.

Another important consideration in this category is the representation of the sexes in your illustration. If you are rendering a couple realistically, as in the illustration at right, then you will automatically indicate a man and a woman (or a boy and girl if you are doing a card for teens). If a different styling is used and you are depicting the couple through two animals, as shown in the illustration of the two teddy bears, flowers, or perhaps birds flying off into the setting sun, give some consideration to how you're going to indicate which is male and which is female (otherwise it could look more like Friendship). Making one smaller than the other is the frequent solution to this problem since women are more often the slighter or shorter of the partners.

Animals representing the couple are an excellent solution because then the specific physical characteristics of the actual couple are avoided. Color of hair, kind of build, degrees of attractiveness, and race are all set aside. If you use the two birds flying off into the setting sun, you then have an entirely appropriate symbol for every couple everywhere of the ideal perfection of their ever-lasting love.

The following step-by-step demonstration is an excellent example of using a couple of cute koala bears to illustrate Romantic Love.

Saying "I love you"
is so much more
than an expression of our feelings . . .
It's a two-way commitment
between hearts . . .
between lives . . .
It's not expecting too much
from each other too soon
but taking time to build our relationship
on trust and respect . . .
It's recognizing our differences
as well as our similarities,
and seeing those differences as a way
to complement each other . . .
It's accepting each other's shortcomings
but emphasizing the strengths,
encouraging the successes
but still loving during the failures . . .

This is an excellent example of a couple rendered realistically so that they might be anybody, with any color of hair or eyes. This makes the card appropriate for a greater number of Romantic Love sending situations.

It's realizing that the things
that make each of us special and unique
also make our relationship
special and unique . . .
It's being friends . . .
liking each other as well, as
loving each other . . .
It's remembering
that even though we're close
we each deserve distance,
that even though we're together,
we each deserve our solitude . . .
It's sharing the sad and happy
the wrong and right
the worst and best . . .
and through everything
still believing that "I love you"
is worth it all

This illustration is a good example of the use of the heart motif in Romantic Love. Note the imaginative solution to the problem presented by the gender identification of Whimsical animals, here accomplished through the use of tiny personal accessories. This solution adds tremendously to the Whimsy and charm of the card.

Love you

It's possible to achieve a very light, delicate effect with colored pencils that is completely suited to the feel and emotional appeal of Romantic Love greeting cards. In this example of using colored pencils (not to be confused with pastel pencils) the style is Whimsical (which will be discussed in Chapter 2). There is no editorial (the verse or prose) on the cover it's just two koala bears hugging. Inside, the card says "We're the best." This card will work for Anniversary as well as numerous small sending situations that pop up at any time in any close relationship.

1

2

3

4

1. *Sketch two animals hugging. Because this is a Whimsical styling you must take liberties with the animal's characteristics to make them slightly ironic, a little silly, sweet, and very lovable to show Romantic Love.*

2. *Here her nose is smaller. The top of her profile is straighter, making her look less pig-like. Her ear has changed.*

3. *Her entire snout is shorter and her original ear is back. Sweater patterns have been introduced. The heart motif is added to reinforce the love message and to enhance the Whimsical charm of the design.*

Now consider your color palette. One of the limitations of this medium is that you have only those colors manufactured as pencils.

You can overlap some colors to change them, but only in a limited way. Consider this when planning your design. Experiment with various combinations of colors until you find ones you particularly like.

4. *Determine the size of the card if you haven't already. Transfer your sketch to the paper on which you intend to do your finish. A rougher textured paper is particularly good for this technique because the tooth of the paper will enhance the soft personality of your pencilwork.*

Taking advantage of the paper's texture, very lightly *fill in the furry areas of the koala bears. Using short, light strokes, create a fuzzy edge around both of them. Use slightly longer strokes for their ear hair.*

5. *Now carefully begin to deepen the brown to add shaping around the edges. Bring some yellow tones (very lightly) in the lighter brown areas, some pink in the ears and cheeks for cuteness, and another level of darkening in the brown areas to suggest a three-dimensional quality.*

6. *Fill in the noses with solid black ink. Do the eyes and mouth with a darker shade of brown. Lightly color in the basic color of each sweater.*

If you like a very light, sketchy feeling, there is absolutely nothing wrong with stopping right here. The situation communicates and evokes a mood. Or you can go a step further for more depth and detail and a greater sense of absurdity, which will only add to the charm of this Whimsical design.

7. *Finally add detail in the sweaters. Overall, come back in and darken and deepen selectively to set off those parts of the design that you would like to be more prominent. Add a hint of color for the baseline.*

Since this is a simple spot design, no further embellishments are necessary to communicate Romantic Love. Go over your entire design lightly with a kneaded eraser. Your original lead pencil lines will come out, and the color will remain.

5

6

7

WEDDING

The person giving or sending this kind of card is congratulating, supporting, or acknowledging the marriage of two people. The card will almost always depict wedding-related subjects: The bride and groom actually being married (that is, standing together) perhaps under a romantic arbor. The bride, when shown, should be in a traditional gown and/or veil, the groom a tuxedo. Many styles of design (see Chapter 2) will work for this sending situation. Illustrating the wedding cake (or knife) works well. Also flowers (often roses), ribbons, wedding bells, two hearts, birds, doves (two of almost anything relating to each other, in combination with the other subjects), glasses of champagne—all these are right for the occasion. And as is always the case, anything new that you can think of that seems right. This is always the challenge of working in greeting cards in general—creating something new that works well!

Degrees of formality are a matter of taste, and sometimes, the closeness in the relationship between the sender of the card and the recipients is a factor. If you don't wish to literally depict a bride and groom, it's perfectly acceptable to use the editorial as the predominant design element. Any other design element used now becomes minor or complementary.

Simple, subtle borders are popular in this case. Pale blue is as good as white. Both imply formality and are very general in their appeal.

Few risks are taken within this category because most (the sixties trend notwithstanding) opt for a *very* traditional wedding today. So, therefore, goes everything related to the occasion. An interesting recent development within Wedding is the tremendous popularity that Wedding Congratulations cards done in Whimsical and Sweetly Charming stylings are enjoying. These stylings are described in Chapter 2.

CONGRATULATIONS

This sending situation encompasses the more general kind of congratulations where the person receiving the card is being commended for an achievement, a piece of good luck, or any good thing that may have happened. This situation is General Congratulations (as opposed to Wedding, just examined, and Baby later in the chapter). The person sending the card is acknowledging the good fortune of the person receiving the card. In this sense the card should be very positive, very upbeat.

The use of an animated person, character, or animal in a celebratory mood to indicate that the person sending the card is very happy, excited, or joyful about the good fortune of the other person is good here. This kind of Congratulations would be good for a new job, a promotion within an old job, winning an award, finishing a project, getting into a school, getting elected to office, winning the lottery. The possibilities are endless. The literally enthusiastic approach is right for a friend or close relationship.

An even broader appeal would be editorial like "Congratulations" on the cover and perhaps "This couldn't have happened to a more deserving person" or "Please accept this congratulations" on the inside. Style the card in such a way that the quote is the predominant design element (see Chapter 8). This approach is so broad that the greeting card would be appropriate for an extremely wide range of Congratulations sending situations. However, it is also less warm. It would be appropriate for sending in less intimate circumstances that Friendship—perhaps a co-worker, a boss, or an acquaintance.

BABY CONGRATULATIONS

This category has recently experienced an expansion in popularity due to the "echo" effect of many baby boom children now reaching their prime child-bearing years. This kind of card congratulates parents on their new baby. It is crucially important to show baby-related elements (toys, bassinets, bottles, high chairs) or a baby. These cards are usually styled in Sweetly Charming or Whimsical ways (there is an opportunity for Humor here as well) and almost always are designed in soft pastel colors (see Chapter 6 for more on baby colors). The illustration, shown right, shows an excellent use of baby elements. The focal point is a vulnerable, sleeping baby and hearts to evoke an affectionate response.

The gender of the baby whose arrival is being celebrated is an important consideration. If the baby is a boy, then the color blue should predominate. If a girl, then pink. Sometimes the sender won't know what the gender of the baby is. How close the relationship between the sender and the parent(s) has a lot to do with this. How well informed the sender is also has some impact. Or you may simply want *your* baby card to work for all eventualities. In this case creating a design with mostly yellow is a good solution. Also a multi-color look with neither pink nor blue predominating will work.

Because the person sending the card is congratulating the happy parents or welcoming the new baby, the use of "big-little" to denote mother and baby can be used. This can be done with either animals or people and in any style. Softer styles have historically been selected the most. Sweetly Charming animals done correctly will always be popular because through their use the situation becomes feminine and idealized. The illustration shown far right, has been designed in this manner. Neither the mother nor the baby is specifically described in human terms so the card can be sent to many different kinds of parents. The warmth and adorableness of the setting are clearly communicated.

The baby in this Baby Congratulations card is shown in an idealized setting. The cradle, picture on the wall, and carpet all say "caring" through the use of the heart motif. The moon seems to stand guard, protecting the baby's vulnerability. These highly effective devices elicit a similar response from the viewer, all very appropriate to the Baby category.

The use of big and little animals together to depict a parent and baby has a strong history of success and increase the card's appeal and send-ability. The timeless warmth and affection shown here are just right for Baby Congratulations.

May your lives together
always be full of love.

Congratulations

Congratulations on your tiny new joy!

21

JUVENILE

Any card intended for a child belongs in this category. Most often these are Birthday cards. Everything pertinent to Birthday is also pertinent here with a few additional concerns. Usually for Juvenile designs the images should be fun and fantastic, anything that you think a child would be delighted to see. Often animals are used. Clowns also work. Animating an otherwise inanimate object like a train or a plane, trees or flowers is an entertaining approach. Whatever your selected subject matter, it should be relatively large on the card. The message should be simple and the lettering should be large and easy to read. Lettering like that used in a child's reader is good (see the illustration on page 11).

The age of the child for whom the card is intended affects the styling used. The look should be softer and sweeter, the younger the child, bolder and brighter the older the child. Also consider the age of the child when selecting subjects. Use subjects you know a child in the age range pertinent to your design would like.

Keep the gender of the child in mind at all times. If the card is intended for a boy, then use images you think would be more fun for a boy. The same applies for cards intended for little girls.

ANNIVERSARY

In this category are really two smaller categories. The first and larger of these is General Anniversary. This is the situation in which the sender of the card wishes to commemorate any Anniversary *other than* a Wedding. A fellow employee, boss, or your own employee could be having an employment Anniversary. Or a club membership may be reaching a landmark or any special thing that may have happened for any person could be reaching its annual celebration. For this type of rememberance, the more general the design, the better. There are so many specific possiblities, each far too small to be literally depicted.

A good solution here is to let the editorial predominate. The cover could say something like "Happy Anniversary" and the inside "May this one be the happiest yet." Such a card works for any of the situations we've just outlined and more. If you use colors that are neither too masculine nor too feminine (see Chapter 6) and use your editorial as the focal point, then your card will work for many different kinds of General Anniversaries.

The other Anniversary category is Wedding. Here the person sending the card is helping the couple commemorate the Anniversary of their Wedding. Illustrate two of anything (people, flowers, animals) to symbolize the couple. Think of this as partly comprised of Romantic Love modified to be appropriate for a Wedding Anniversary. The more general approach just outlined, with the editorial as the focal point, also works here. The 25th and 50th Wedding Anniversary are characterized by the use of a metallic silver and gold respectively. These kinds of greeting cards are usually very formal and very traditional.

GET WELL/CHEER

Cheer cards should be bright and uplifting. This card is sent to someone who is or has been unwell to let that person know that he or she is being thought of and wished well. It is most important in this situation to concentrate of the state of mind of the recipient of the card. Only positive, encouraging, and supportive images should be used. Each flower must look fresh and new, for example, with never a hint of wilt or dying. Within this context, any style is appropriate.

SYMPATHY

This sending situation is a very delicate one. This card is sent to let the bereaved know that they are thought of during their time of loss. The card should offer condolences. The design should be muted and tranquil, not depressing. White or pale blue works well. Understated florals and simple borders are also very good. This is one category where experimentation in styles and approaches should be conservative. Traditional approaches work best as no one wants to risk offense.

THANK YOU

This is not a large category, so it's a good idea to design each card in such a way that it can be all things to all people. The occasion might be an instance where a neighbor helped out while your car was in the shop or a friend dropped off a favorite book for you to read or a gift was given and greatly appreciated. You may simply have been a luncheon or dinner guest. Thank you cards are usually light and non-specific, but keep the full range of possibilities in mind. The illustration with flowers shown opposite, is a good example of a general Thank You. The following step-by-step demonstration shows how to create a very general Thank You card using an airbrush.

In this chapter you've examined the major sending situations for greeting cards. They have not necessarily been discussed in order of popularity. Different regions, different environments, all kinds of factors influence popularity. Generally, Friendship and Birthday are the most popular and the rest are approximately equal, with Sympathy perhaps trailing a little behind the others. Popularity shifts with changing social trends as well. Some categories pointed out as growing now might either continue to grow or begin to shift in other ways. You can keep aware of these shifts by researching social trends. See Chapter 9.

After studying these sending situations, you will begin to see some of the possibilities inherent in combining situations. For example, you can combine Religious with almost any other situation and create a whole new one: Religious Birthday, Religious Wedding, Religious Baby Congratulations, Religious Thank You. Or you might combine Romantic Love with Birthday, Anniversary, or Get Well, and so on.

Each sending situation can be further divided into relative versions as well: Mother Birthday, Aunt Get Well. The more specific each category becomes, however, the fewer people the card is right for. If you are planning on illustrating each and every card yourself and you don't care about mass production, then you'll probably know in advance who you'll be sending each card to. The point about broad sendability won't matter to you at all. But the moment any sort of commercial application or mass production becomes a possibility, then you should begin to pay particular attention to this entire area. Commercially, you will want each card to be right for the greatest number of people possible. Your card will then have the greatest number of sales and thus be judged a success.

A very simple editorial combined with bright, red flowers and a light airy feeling make this card just right for a very general Thank You.

Thank You

The cover of the card will say, "thank you" and the inside will say, "Thank you for your thoughtfulness." The editorial will be the focal point of the cover design and you will work in a Stylized Graphic manner so this card may be as general in appeal as possible. On pages 131–132 in Chapter 8 you can see in detail the steps through which the lettering was created.

There are so many effects you can achieve with an airbrush. In this example you will be taking advantage of the wonderful softness that only an airbrush can create. You will also examine the use of liquid masks and raised paper masks.

1

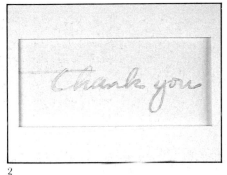

2

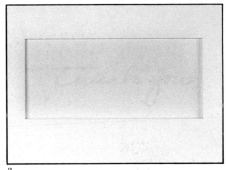

3

4

1. *Because of the many and various complexities involved in working with an airbrush, it's important to think through your design carefully in advance.*

You know that your subject matter is editorial. Try out several possibilities as thumbnail (meaning tiny) sketches. Select the one that seems best.

In this case a border is in keeping with the very general look you want. Your colors will be blue and burgundy, simple and neutral.

2. *Determine the size of your card, sketch in the border, and transfer the lettering onto the paper on which you will do your finish. Remember to use crop marks and to bleed the background color since it will extend to the edges of the card.*

Carefully paint in the lettering with liquid mask and a nylon brush. Cut a mat that is the

size of your inside border out of a larger piece of paper. Save the center section (you will use it in Step 5). Take three or four pieces of masking tape, make them into rolls with the sticky side out, and place them around the underside of your mat.

Erase the inside border lines on your final sketch and mount the mat lightly on the sketch. Using masking tape and any kind of paper available, mask out the outside edge of the bleed for a neat appearance. This is only important if your work will be sold commercially.

3. *On scrap paper experiment with your airbrush to get a feel for the widths of the spray and the different effects you can create. Also play around with the effect achieved by holding your airbrush at varying distances from the paper.*

Using a wide spray and holding your brush

several inches back from the finished sketch, spray the center area of the design very lightly with blue. The raised mat will give you a very soft edge around the border area.

4. *Wait until the paint is dry. Using a knife and taking care not to cut or tear anything, slowly lift out all the liquid mask over your lettering except the tiny piece extending into the border. It's a good idea to remove the liquid mask as soon as you can after applying it, as it may begin to stick to your paper and become increasingly difficult to remove. Using a kneaded eraser, carefully lift out any pencil lines remaining in the lettering.*

5

6

5. *Again take a few rolled pieces of masking tape with the sticky side out and place them on the mask for the center section (this is the piece you saved in Step 2). Mount the mask lightly over the center area which should be dry now.*

6. *Still using the same blue in a broad spray and keeping the same distance from your paper as before, go back and forth along each edge, lightly at first. Slowly and patiently build layer after layer of blue to deepen the color at the outside edges. Use less color as you near the center. The best way is to go over the surface faster here.*

7. *Wait for the paint to dry. Then remove the center mask and the outside border mat very carefully. Lift the remaining liquid mask out of the tiny piece of lettering under the outside border.*

8. *Now paint the lettering in burgundy. Add horizontal lines to anchor your layout and now you have a Thank You card with a general appeal. The border is soft and the lettering warm, so this design will appeal to men and women.*

7

8

25

BLANK CARDS/POSTCARDS

The last category is both not a sending situation and all sending situations, depending on the use to which the card is put after it's selected. This is the Blank Card. It has no editorial on the inside of the card. The illustration alone either limits or broadens its sendability. That is the advantage of Blank Cards—they can be anything to anyone and are thus highly successful in some environments.

You could, for example, paint a birthday cake design for the cover of the card and put no words on the inside. You would technically have a Blank Card, but you would have limited its sendability to Birthday.

Examine the two illustrations on this page and the top one on the opposite page. Their only limitation is that they are perhaps too Feminine to be sent by or to men. Since most sending of greeting cards takes place among women, that's not a bad limitation.

The disadvantage inherent in Blank Cards is that some people really want greeting cards to speak for them, and the Blank Card doesn't give these people the words they need. However, this category has experienced growth in recent years.

The same advantages and disadvantages apply to Postcards, with an added disadvantage. The message written on the postcard is not private. The illustration of the shells on the bottom of the opposite page is a beautiful example of current postcard art. A lot of humor is being applied to postcards today. This category has also been experiencing growth in recent years.

Published and distributed by Portal Publications, Ltd., Corte Madera, California.

(Above left) This design is delicate, sensitive, and additonally interesting because of its depth of field. It's an elegant Blank Card.

(Left) Blank Cards as a category are enjoying ever-growing popularity. This design is a beautiful example of the use of light to evoke a mood.

Blue Mountain Printmakers/Dona Thompson

(Above) Unique things work for Blank Cards. The situation depicted on this one is delightfully lovely.

(Left) Postcards are experiencing growing popularity. They can be used for any sending situation. This example illustrates a Graphic, yet soft, way of designing with the highly popular sea shell motif. No editorial was used.

The beauty of this Realistic illustration brings out the fragility and grace of these lovely poppies. The delicacy of the foliage and complementary flowers as well as the sensitive and striking use of color all combine to make this a greeting card with great appeal. No editorial was used.

2

ILLUSTRATING IN POPULAR STYLES

IF YOU examine commercial greeting cards, you'll find that everything possible has been done to provide some kind of greeting card for every sending situation and every potential buyer of cards. For this reason there are a lot of different styles of greeting cards. There are far too many to absolutely and inclusively categorize every one. However, this chapter will define some of the broader design styles in general use as greeting cards today.

By examining these very general categories, you will begin to see how you can use your particular way of working to illustrate your own greeting card ideas. Studying these styles will also raise possibilities for further experimentation in areas which you had not previously considered. The important thing to remember is that *whatever* the type of artwork you do, within the wealth of stylistic opportunity open to greeting cards today, there most certainly will be a place for you. Understanding what a greeting card is and what it is supposed to do will equip you to apply your own unique and special look to your greeting cards in an informed and intelligent way, thereby ensuring your success.

REALISTIC

The term "Realistic," as it's used here, is a relative one. What it means is that illustrations styled in this manner are more true to life, more real in the way subjects are depicted than are most illustrations in other styles. For example, the scale of the flowers depicted in the illustration shown on page 28 in relation to their setting is accurate. Few liberties have been taken with the real, physical properties of the subject matter. It is a good example of a Realistic styling.

Not everything included under the heading of this styling should be taken directly and literally from nature or its real origin. It's important not to lose sight of the fact that you, as the artist, are in control. Keeping in mind some of the general considerations raised in Chapter 1, examine your potential greeting card design in such a light. The card must make the recipient feel good and so the card must evoke a mood. If you're looking at real leaves with spots of blight on them or some part of a plant that's rotting or dying, it's best to change those parts of your design in order to keep the feeling upbeat and positive.

The Realistic approach to illustrating greeting cards has a tremendous history of success. If the greeting card that appeals to or pleases the greatest number of people is the greatest success (and in this field it is), then the Realistic approach always wins. It's always safe to send this kind of card to someone. It will threaten none and please many. There is no specific statement of style inherent in this approach that might be misinterpreted by the person receiving the card. It's a safe choice and there are a lot of people who want just that.

Design Realistic Florals and you can't go wrong (unless the editorial goes wrong). The challenge and fun of working within this category are to think of all the ways in which you can add special notes that make your own design unusual and moving. Think of all the things you can do to add to the poetry and delight of each design you undertake.

One very effective tool is the use of light to elicit a response. The illustration on page 58 is an excellent example of a feeling of sweetness, femininity, cleanness, and nostalgia achieved, in part, through the effective use of light. Breezes, color, and subject all combine with this wonderful use of light to produce an effective design. Try juxtaposing unusual combinations of subject matter to tickle one's fancy as in the illustration shown opposite where the delicate, feminine sliver of moon, the partylike flight of balloons, and the tranquil, homey sheep all combine to truly delight. This design is almost a Sophisticated styling, but it is just shy of that category because of the homeyness of the sheep and the farmland.

Adding other, more decorative kinds of design elements in combination with the Realistic style is another interesting approach to try.

What a delightful and fanciful design is this example of a realistically styled Blank Card! The moods evoked are many, ranging from nostalgia to a sense of the absurd. This is an excellent example of just how creative one's approach can be in any category of styling.

❝ My interest in art began when I was very young and I embellished the illustrations in my storybooks to suit *my* idea of how the princess should look. From that time on I have enjoyed a sort of storybook, larger-and-lusher-than-life look in art! Call it the Gild-the-Lily School.

I went to art school for two years right out of boarding school in Canada, but I wasn't interested in drawing as much as boys and dating and getting married, which I did at the age of twenty-one. One of my very first greeting cards was a Christmas card for my husband, a portrait of him from the rear doing the bossa nova, entangled in the Christmas tree lights!

I got serious about art in 1971, following my divorce. My kids were 9 and 12. I won a scholarship to the Academy of Art College in San Francisco and was on my way!

I started collecting kids' books and greeting cards because I was drawn to that kind of artwork. I am attracted to the playful quality in a lot of it, the magical, childlike feeling. Innocence, if you will! People expect me to look about 25 dressed all in gingham. In fact I'm rather a sophisticated middle-aged lady. At least on the outside.

It was difficult at first getting my ideas out there. I lacked money for a decent portfolio and slick presentations and I lacked confidence in my artwork. I was unsure about just what style or direction was truly mine, and for some years, my work was all over the place as far as style. It began to come together and feel *true* when I started painting in acrylics in my spare time, beginning with very clean, simple still life designs and experimenting with color, texture, content, pattern, completely ignoring perspective (a course I had not taken in school, which still terrifies

me!). I loved these paintings. They felt like *my* work. Much of my commercial advertising work did not.

My first real break was a commission to do a series of fruits and vegetables for a card company in Berkeley, California. The cards were quite beautiful, but I was never paid according to my agreement with the owner; the cards were printed with my signature removed. It was a nightmare that I later used as an example for my students of one of the pitfalls to avoid in the greeting card business. But the look was successful and I got other commissions based on that.

I went to conferences, submitted slides all over the place for years, to all the companies I admired. But nothing! There were lots of "we like your work but we already did something like that last year"; as well as lots of requests to work for nothing up front, which I could not afford to do then.

My big break was when John Carroll of Creative Papers by C.R. Gibson, whom I had known professionally for years, asked me to do a series of cards in 1985. It was a dream come true! He used six existing paintings and I created ten new ones for the series. It was the happiest work I had done to date, since he gave me some rough subject suggestions and otherwise a completely free rein. I love doing the work and I guess he liked them too as I have completed a second series of "Heather's World" for Creative Papers by C.R. Gibson. I think this group is better!

I really don't know how my ideas evolve or where I get them. They just sort of pop up and must be expressed. Sometimes it's a group of objects that inspire me; sometimes a combination of colors or just a mood, for example, a wedding will suggest a theme as shown here. I did a lot of experimenting before I got comfortable

with the style I work in now, but that changes rapidly too, since I'm now using watercolor and no acrylic. I suspect one of these days I might even get into some perspective!

If my contribution to the greeting card field is unique, it is with great thanks for inspiration provided by artists such as Lowell Herrero, Charles Wysocki, Etienne Delessert, and Nancy Eckholm Burkert. What I have in common with those artists, and I guess with the people who buy my cards, is a childlike spirit, a joyful warmth of *attitude* that transcends labels. I like the order and beauty of simple, domestic things and creatures as I design them into a moment, a little scene. I like homey, happy, corny stuff. So when they are successful it must be that there are other homey, happy, corny people out there, no matter what daily face they wear for a job and the world at large.

I think one of the nicest things about this line of work is that while I know it's not great art and has absolutely no "real" depth or significance, it does touch people. And the level is friendly, caring, a little bit of "me-to-you" stuff that matters in a busy mechanized world. **❞**

This is an excellent example of a full-bleed design on a Wedding Congratulations card. Almost every possible subject appropriate to the occasion is employed and composed together in a warm, charming, and inviting design.

CONGRATULATIONS

TO YOU BOTH!

Cover editorial

MAY YOU SHARE

MANY HAPPY YEARS TOGETHER!

Inside editorial

SWEETLY CHARMING

You know that women are the predominant senders and receivers of greeting cards. The Sweetly Charming style is traditionally feminine, which makes it an important style category. Almost always the subject matter is animals; sometimes it's people. Whichever is used the key is to stylize, by exaggerating selected characteristics, to make the subject as endearing as possible, as cute as possible. The job is easier if you begin with something that is already perceived to be sweet, like a teddy bear and kitty. When you design for this category, you are creating a small fantasy world in which all is sweetly serious. These cards are a form of escape, almost like an adult fairy tale.

The ultimate point is to make the person receiving the card feel good. Sweetly Charming stylings should elicit an "Oh, how darling!" kind of response, a tugging at the heartstrings. Tininess also works as part of this formula as in the cozy illustration shown right. This styling personifies the most traditional concepts of femininity. The exaggerated fluffiness of the kitty, its huge tail, tiny eyes, and big pink nose all emphasize sweetness and endearment. This is Sweetly Charming at its daintiest. Many, many women respond to it.

The illustration of the bunnies, shown far right, is another example of a design done in the Sweetly Charming manner. The eyes are beautiful and soft. The gesture of the couple is sweet in its innocence. Indeed, the entire concept of a flower-filled gondola in a country setting under a full moon is an excellent example of the childlike (not to be confused with childish) quality of innocence that is an important part of this style.

As you can see, there are many ways of achieving a Sweetly Charming styling. Yours should be entirely different. That's what's so interesting about designing and illustrating greeting cards. There's so much variety! Use the points raised here to help you understand the general parameters of the style, the whys of its success, and develop your own unique version of it. Play with various subjects, exaggerate features, and then examine the results.

BY: M. © MELCHER

Thinking warm and pleasant thoughts

...thinking of you...

This is an excellent example of a Sweetly Charming design. The use of tininess, vulnerability, fluffiness, and hominess all work together to evoke an emotional response.

This is an excellent example of the Sweetly Charming style. Note the simplicity and innocence of the gesture shared by the couple and yet feel the intimacy implied by their closeness. This also uses a wonderful light to enhance the warmth and romantic quality of the situation.

Happy Anniversary!

WHIMSICAL

This manner of working is very close to Sweetly Charming in some ways. The look is similar and the feel is most definitely feminine, but not quite so completely and traditionally. Everything that is true about Sweetly Charming is also true about Whimsical except that where Sweetly Charming is serious, Whimsical is *very slightly* funny or ironic or silly. Whimsical leans a tad toward the Humorous area. Just look at this illustration and study this wonderfully absurd cat done in such a delicate and feminine way. The situation is disarming in its strangeness. It's not a "ho, ho" funny kind of card. This is something that sneaks up on you and sort of tickles as well as it charms. It's Whimsical.

It's possible that this category fills a need for the "new" woman. The woman who is a little put off by traditional concepts of femininity, but is still essentially feminine in her outlook. She wants something more emotionally delicate than many Humorous cards (see Chapter 5) and less fussy than most Sweetly Charming cards. Whimsical is a very successful look.

The understated exuberance of the girl and her teddy in the illustration shown opposite creates a delightful sense of fantasy. The sheer fun and silliness of this design move it away from Sweetly Charming and into Whimsical.

Depicting the couple in an unflattering, yet charming, stance in the illustration on page 38 and then surrounding them with traditional symbols of Wedding, creates an irresistible tickling appeal. Childlike simplicity is working here. It's also at work in the illustration of the wash basin on page 39 where a totally different approach still results in Whimsy.

Study both Sweetly Charming *and* Whimsical, understand the difference (a *light* touch of irony, humor, wit, and silliness) between Whimsical and its sweeter counterpart, and begin to work to make Whimsical your own. Use those things you do best. Adapt them to make your work even more charming and irresistible.

THE WAITING CAT

I haven't moved a whisker
since you left!

Hurry back!

Elements of totally charming absurdity like the cat's posture and absolutely wonderful slippers, the topiary shrubs outside, and the portrait on the wall all combine to make this a terrific example of a Whimsical styling.

This Whimsical styling is particularly effective because of the charming understatement of the exuberance of the girl and teddy bear. Note the delightful addition of tiny teddies in each corner of the border.

Kick up your heels and
have a wonderful birthday!

Penguins with silly grins, one wearing a top hat and tie, the other a veil and pearls, both in a squat wide-legged stance surrounded by heart-shaped balloons, are just the right kind of charming absurdity for a Whimsical greeting card.

You were meant for each other.
Wishing you all the best!

Dream your dreams...

FLAVIA

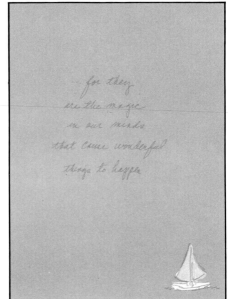

...for they are the magic in our minds that cause wonderful things to happen

This example achieves the Whimsical not through a sense of light humor or irony, but rather through a sense of the fantastic and magical. An other-worldly quality accomplishes the same things in a different and very beautiful way.

SHAWN MORY MCMILLION

"From my earliest memory I remember drawing. I drew anything and everything, but especially I loved drawing animals because I love animals with a passion. I was the oldest of five children. My mother was divorced and supported us with some assistance from her widowed grandmother. Money was something that was never in abundance around our house, but love and creativity were. My mother would go to the local newspaper, get the end-rolls of newsprint, tape it to the lower half of our walls, and let the five of us have a field day drawing on the walls.

Art was a very big factor in my growing up for a number of reasons. Probably the biggest influence came from my hometown of Laguna Beach, California: a world-renowned artist colony. The multitude of galleries helped my mother provide us with an abundance of free entertainment and I enjoyed seeing all the beautiful and different styles and mediums of fine art. Years later, as a single parent I took my own daughter, Jessica, to the same galleries that I frequented as a child.

Every summer we went to the three art festivals that ran all summer. Later, as a teenager I worked as an usher at the Pageant of the Masters: a life-size tableau of works by the classic painters enacted by people standing in for subjects of the painting. Every night for six weeks I would watch 20 or 30 tableaus of fantastic art come to life before me and it never occurred to me that kids everywhere didn't grow up with this as well. I took art for granted because it was everywhere in my life.

Being an artist wasn't something that I ever thought I'd do; being an artist was something that I was. Initially I didn't plan to study anything, having married right out of high school and become a young mother. But that marriage failed quickly and I found myself single, with a young daughter to support and not a whole lot of direction. I did everything and anything. All the jobs added immensely to my powers of observation about life, people, experiences, and feelings.

Eventually I got a job as an Animal Services Officer. It was an incredible experience for me because I was being paid to work with and care for animals. I was proud to be a major part of the first pro-life animal rescue and management organization in the country. Part of our service was to educate members of the community about responsible animal care and on occasion I would speak to various school and civic groups. I gave out flyers that frequently contained my illustrations. Because money was tight I also drew pictures for gifts for my family and friends. I carried an ink pen around with a sketch pad and during my coffeebreaks I would draw.

Sometimes in our lives there comes a turning point, a fork in the road, when a special person makes us see in ourselves what they see in us. That one special person in my life was Neil J. Purcell, then my Captain and currently the Chief of Police at Laguna Beach. I was on a break one day and, as usual, working on a pen-and-ink drawing for a friend. Captain Purcell came into the briefing room and wanted to know what I was doing. I was bashful but I showed him my drawing pad containing several drawings in various stages of completion. He was impressed; he asked if I had ever attempted to jury into any of the art festivals. It turned out the Neil and his wife, Michelle, were both seriously involved with the Art-A-Fair Festival of Arts in Laguna Beach; he was a board member and an artist. He told me how to mat and frame my pictures and that the jury was four weeks away, so I had plenty of time to prepare. To make a long story short, I juried and got accepted at the Festival. My drawings were simple pen and inks of animals and plants. But I felt like Picasso! Never while I was growing up could I have imagined that I would be showing my own art at the same festivals I had attended with great regularity and admiration.

I got my booth set up and my artwork framed and hung for display and I invited everyone whom I knew from my rounds as an Animal Services Officer to the opening of the Art-A-Fair. On the day of the grand opening, while I was on patrol in my animal truck I was rear-ended by a cement truck carrying 27 tons of asphalt going 40 miles an hour—and the course of my life changed forever.

I missed the opening. And I ended up in a coma for two months, I coudn't focus my eyes for almost a year, was in and out of rehabilitation for two years, and my employment with the city was terminated because I was unable to do the job. But believe it or not, that accident was one of the best things that ever happened to me! (Though I didn't exactly think so at the time!)

Because I couldn't focus my eyes to do the pen work, I started painting with watercolors. The reason I chose watercolors wasn't based on any artistic genius. Rather, they were cheap (for someone on disability that was a major consideration!), didn't smell, and were quick to clean up. As my focus gradually returned, I started combining pen and ink with watercolor and to this day I still do that.

Losing my job of security, regular paychecks, and insurance benefits made me take stock of my life's choices. If I was struggling to make it with a job and overtime, I might as well struggle to make it as an artist. I waited on tables, and Jessica and I went door-to-door, selling three floral notecards that I had made. We earned a dollar for each package of 9, including envelopes! Even when I worked two jobs at the same time, I still came home and squeezed in a couple of hours each night for painting. I went into card shops and copied the names and addresses of various companies off of the backs of cards, then submitted my art to them. For three and a half years I got rejections from everybody.

Jessica and I would go to local art shows and receive comments, criticism, and suggestions from the public. I painted this incredibly beautiful frog with some flowers and no one would buy it. I couldn't understand it! Finally I asked several people. They said that most people didn't hang frogs in their houses. I learned by listening to the public what they did like; what subjects, colors, layouts, themes. I still encourage comments and suggestions.

The public has a lot of good, constructive information to contribute and I feel strongly about tapping into their feelings. The more I listened to the public the more successful I became in selling my paintings to them. I taught myself to draw, to paint watercolors, and to make embossment and etchings. I asked a zillion questions of every artist I met who would talk to me, and I made at least two zillion mistakes along the way.

Finally Steven Mack of the C.R. Gibson Company decided to take a chance on me. As a freelancer I sold one card to them called "Eliza Duck." After I had designed for C.R. Gibson for several years as a freelancer, with several of my designs selling quite well, Steven Mack decided to give me a contract. Not being a trained artist in some ways was a help. I didn't have any phobias about doing anything unconventional. In other ways it was a hindrance, because I didn't know how to do any of the technical work.

I started to take a graphic arts program at a community college, but six weeks into the course I moved to another state. In the new community I bluffed my way into a graphic arts assistant job. Whenever I didn't know how to do a specific task, such as paste-up, I would just ask the guy in charge, "Well just how did you want this done?" and he would tell me. I got a great education to boot in layout and camera work.

Under the direction of John Carroll at C.R. Gibson my greeting card line has really grown. Designing for a company is a team effort and we both put ideas and suggestions in as well as taking them out. I know the characters that I draw to a T and I have confidence to say when I don't think they should be in a certain situation. I would also be unreasonable if I didn't take the C.R. Gibson staff's ideas and expand on them. It's like a marriage; we both put our best into it for the good of the relationship and we both deserve the credit for its success. I will be the one who gets the lion's share of the credit for the popularity of any of the designs that I've done, but I owe a debt of gratitude to the behind-the-scenes people who helped me get here. It's important to be professional but I don't take myself too seriously. Profes-

sionalism is working with the staff to conceptualize a line, executing it neatly and on time and not being too filled with your own self-importance when it hits the market. I remarried several years ago; Gregg Carlson is a wonderful man and the three of us have a great life. Designing cards won't make you rich monetarily but as far as life's choices, it's a wonderful way to live. We never quite know where our next house payment is coming from, but we all work together and it's fun!

The success of my cards comes from a culmination of many factors: sweetness, humor, animation, spontaneity, sensitivity, and the unexpected. My ideas are how I want the world to be, rather than the way it is. Teddy bears don't really give Valentines and geese don't really go to birthday parties; but it sure would be fun if they did! I'm a firm believer that everything you do in life adds to your awareness and sensitivities and compassion. The struggles that I endured helped to shape my ideas, feelings, style, and subjects. Life can be very hard for a lot of people and if I can make them smile for just a moment with one of my cards, it's worth it. I've translated my love of animals into my drawn animals. It's their facial expressions that make them so successful. They really come to life on the page and people sense that.

It's important for others in the business who are struggling to get their foot in the door to know that there are alternate ways to get into designing besides art school. I love what I do and honestly feel that I'm the luckiest girl alive to be doing what I do the way I do it. Through my art I'm able to make the lives of other people a little nicer, and I can't think of a better way to live. **"**

The Country French influence is apparent in this warm and loving design by Shawn Mory McMillion. Color, style, and subject matter all combine to underscore the extreme femininity and innate appeal of this wonderful Birthday card. The Country French influence is discussed in depth on page 44.

wishing you loads of warm birthday hugs!

HUMOROUS

Any manner of working that makes people laugh belongs in the Humorous group. Chapter 5 contains an outline of some devices you can use to make a card funny. The category is included here as well to remind you that it does exist in the general context of greeting cards. Don't overlook the possibilities inherent in this area. It's a very important one today because lately it's experienced the largest growth of any area of greeting cards. This is where it's happening today in greeting cards.

You may have some tendencies or inclinations that could be adapted to Humorous Cards and not even know it! You may think that you or your work isn't funny. Consider for a moment the birthday illustration shown right. At a glance you would probably call this a Whimsical card. It's not. Read the editorial and you'll see that this greeting card is definitely Humorous and only *looks* Whimsical. The illustration of the man with four arms shown opposite, is another matter entirely. This is a very funny card and you know it the moment you see it.

This whole area is very important. If you're interested in it be sure to spend some time on Chapter 5 for more information about how to do these kinds of cards.

It should be taken with
six bags of potato chips,
one quart of onion dip,
three bowls of popcorn
and two pounds
of assorted chocolates!

A birthday should not be taken lightly!

This example looks like a Whimsical card, but the editorial is distinctly Humorous. If you keep in mind that most greeting cards are sent and received by women you will rarely go wrong.

You're really different!

Perhaps more so than is necessary.

This Humorous design is funny in a most straightforward manner. There is humor in the artwork itself and then the editorial goes the art one better, creating a greeting card that is even funnier than you first believed it was going to be.

Anything that doesn't fall into one of the previous four styles of working falls into the Stylized category. In general, the look here is "newer." The categories you've just examined (*not* the examples shown) have been around in one form or another since greeting cards originated as we know them in modern American life. Their popularity is pretty much assured. Tastes and issues may change superficially, but the things people want to say to one another don't change fundamentally.

It should be emphasized that the looks classified under Stylized are *newer*, not less successful. Some of the very newest are riskier because they don't have a strong history of sales, but this is not true of *all* the types included under Stylized.

Each most certainly has its own following and in each case it's a strong one. That's why they're included here. Keep in mind, though, that the appeal of each may or may not be as broad as the appeal of the first four styles you examined earlier in this chapter.

AMERICAN COUNTRY/
COUNTRY FRENCH

Because women buy so many greeting cards the American Country look does very, very well. It's the single, most popular, long-standing home decorating look in this country (an earlier form was Early American). In a way it *is* this country. It's derived directly from the American heritage. Women are comfortable with it. Country French shares this characteristic. They are both safe, warm, and cozy. If the woman to whom you are sending a card is into a Country look in her home, then you can feel cer-

tain that the design shown in the illustration of the teddy bear and duck, page 41, for example, would please her. As would the illustration of the rustic basket with flowers, shown opposite, which is an excellent example of American Country. Examine the illustration of the rural scene, below. It's a wonderful example of the primitivism that is the cornerstone of this type of card.

This is an extremely important area of Stylized greeting card art and one of the two most popular under the Stylized heading. If you find you are attracted to Country, begin now to explore ways you can make it your own unique statement. Read Chapter 9 carefully to learn about ways to research the looks and subject matter most characteristic of this type of card. The following step-by-step demonstration illustrates how to execute an American Country design using gouache.

This American Country styling has a contemporary flair. The woman who is into Country will feel completely comfortable with this Blank Card.

(Left)
This Blank Card is a rich and warm example of classic American Country. The hominess and wealth of detail in this primitively rendered rural scene evoke a mood that is cozy and nostalgic.

DEMONSTRATION THREE

STYLING

AN AMERICAN

COUNTRY DESIGN

IN GOUACHE

In this example of using gouache the style is American Country and the sending situation is Friendship, Thinking of You. The cover will say, "Thoughts of you . . ." and the inside ". . . are always welcome." Since the welcome wreath is synonymous with Country, it works beautifully with the editorial. You may want to research Country wreath designs using sources noted in Chapter 9.

Gouache is a kind of water-based paint that has a number of advantages. It can be either opaque or translucent, its color range is extensive and its colors are bright and uplifting, all of which make it an appropriate choice for an American Country card.

1. *Do a rough thumbnail sketch of your design to get an idea of how you see it coming together.*

2. *Determine the size of your greeting card and begin working on your sketch at this size. A border layout is used here. Because of the symmetrical nature of the design, make careful measurements to be certain all the design elements will fit. Using your rough sketch, transfer the drawing to the paper on which you will be doing your finish. This is your final drawing and you will be painting directly on it. Because of this, be sure to keep your pencil lines light and delicate. Note that in addition to the welcome wreath, hearts have been added for more warmth and charm.*

3. *Consider your color palette: yellow, pink, lavender, green, teal, and blue. You will be combining translucent and opaque color. Where you want greater opacity (as in the yellow, green, and lavender), simply add white. Where you want translucency (as in the teal and blue), add water. Paint in the darker teal first. The watered color gives a mottled effect that adds to the crafted look desired in American Country stylings. After this color dries, lift out the pencil lines around it with your kneaded eraser.*

4. *One color at a time, paint in each additional color, beginning with the pink. Then add the blue and lavender. Erase all remaining linework in the design.*

5. *Finally come in with the opaque yellow in the backround of the center area. Paint the yellow in carefully. You will need a tiny no. 00000 brush to get around the lettering and wreath. Now your design is finished.*

1

2

3

4

Thoughts of you ...

5

ORIENTAL

This is a classic and very elegant design style that has been enjoying success in greeting cards for about the last ten years. It is the second of the two most popular categories of Stylized greeting cards. The artforms have existed for centuries and if you are interested in this manner of working, historical research is a must. The most frequently used subjects are birds and Florals. The illustration of flowers is a beautiful example of the latter. There is a lot of value in this look. The grace and elegance of the styling say that this is something special, something a little dressy to send to a friend or aquaintance.

Each morning is like being reborn...

we get another chance
to be
the best
that we can be.

Spontaneity, the appearance of ease, and evidence of the artist's hand are all characteristic of the Oriental style. Certain characteristic design layouts are also important. Each of these elements is gracefully illustrated in this example.

GRAPHIC

The Graphic look is a clean, flat one. It's general in its appeal. This means that it will be right for men as well as women. This approach is bright, bold, active, and sometimes even soft. Frequently abstract, nonrepresentational images are used. Nothing literal is illustrated, just a feeling, each distinct in itself. Often the editorial is featured as the major design element. This bold illustration of an ice cream cone does depict specific subject matter but in a flat, linear, Graphic style.

In this manner of working experimentation can be a lot of fun. Many newer looks for greeting cards are introduced through this category and succeed. It is constantly shifting and changing.

The following step-by-step demonstration shows how the Graphic style can be used to create an exciting graduation card using gouache.

Happy Birthday

It's bold, it's Graphic, and it evokes a mood. Who can fail to respond to the fun feeling of an ice cream cone, polka dots, and brilliant magenta? The result is positive and upbeat.

USING GOUACHE
TO CREATE
A GRAPHIC
GRADUATION CARD

It's important that this Graphic card work for many general graduation situations, so the colors should be general, the mood celebratory. The mortarboard is an excellent symbol of graduation. There is no editorial on the cover and the inside will say "What an achievement! Congratulations Graduate!" The medium used here is gouache.

1. *Work on your sketch. Tossed caps are a wonderful way to communicate the exultant mood of the occasion. Develop a color palette. Because of the very general nature of a Graphic card, a blue background is just right. It also represents specific subject matter—sky. The color of the mortarboards should be neutral, with bright spots of confetti to spark the design with color as well as add to the festive mood.*

2. *Transfer your sketch to the paper on which you're doing your finish. When you mix your colors, add white for a certain opacity since you're working on a colored background. Mix each color thoroughly. Add water if necessary to thin. Your paint should be about the consistency of honey. Begin by painting in the middle beige of all the mortarboards.*

3. *Go into the mortarboards with the lighter beige to highlight key areas like the tassles and strings.*

4. *Now go back into the mortarboards with the darker beige to accent additonal areas and achieve a three-dimensional feel.*

5. *Paint all the confetti in the background in each of the remaining colors and your festive Graphic design is completed.*

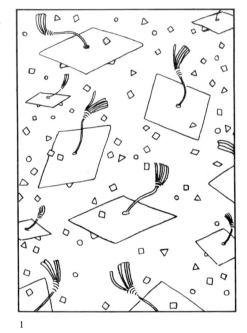

1

2

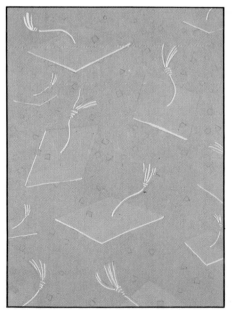

3

4

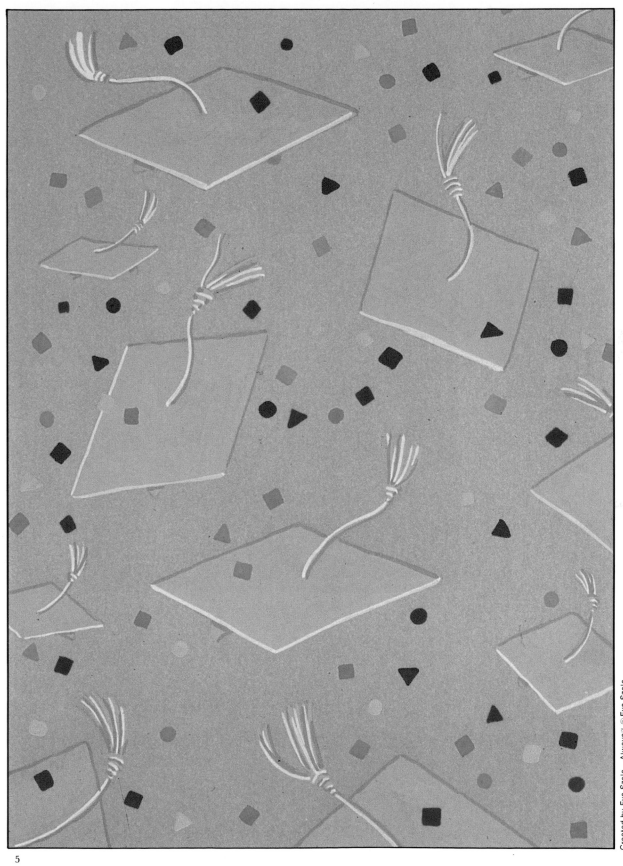

Sophisticated is possibly the narrowest in appeal of all the styles in this category. And yet if you're interested in a commercial application of your work, this is sometimes the area of greatest interest (next to Humorous) for many distributors. The industry is always looking for something new. In recent years that is most often a Sophisticated look or a Humorous approach. The challenge of working within the Sophisticated style is to be new and timely, even trendy. But always keep in mind all the things that characterize a successful greeting card and try to bring as much of that to working in this manner as you can. For example, the illustration of the black cat, shown on page 55, is an extremely elegant design, very upscale in feeling, but it takes no chances with subject matter. Cats are among the very most popular of subjects and almost always enjoy success. This is the way to take risks: Try something new along with something tried and true.

The illustration shown right is most assuredly about and for women. It's a fresh, new, and delightful look in the world of greeting cards. The illustration shown opposite is an excellent sample of a Graphic card that is categorized as Sophisticated because of its extremely upscale, top-of-the-line look. While these types of stylings may not have broad followings, when they do find their respective niches, their fans are loyal and demanding. The woman who wants Sophisticated usually wants nothing else. The recent popularity of Art Deco is part of this phenomenon. The following step-by-step demonstration is a good example of how to use black and white artwork to design a very exciting, sophisticated greeting card.

GO EASY & IF YOU CAN'T GO EASY

go as easy
as
you
can
.

Gertrude Stein

This is an interesting, new, fresh-looking Sophisticated look. The handling of color and layout and the terrifically fun (and still pertinent) approach to the editorial all contribute to the elegance of this greeting card.

The dynamic energy and light feeling of this very Sophisticated design combine to create a completely new and very special Graphic look.

Wishes
Were kisses,
you'd be covered
With them!
Happy Birthday

DESIGNING A SOPHISTICATED CARD WITH BLACK AND WHITE ART

There is a lot of black and white designing going on in greeting cards today in the Alternative markets. (See Chapter 5 for a discussion of this subject.) This is an exciting area where you can have a lot of fun and let your creativity run free. Just be sure to keep the purpose of your greeting card in mind. In this example it's general Friendship. The editorial on the cover is "Hi" and there is no copy on the inside of the card. You will use ink and patterned film to create a very Sophisticated styling.

1. *There are so many exciting and inspiring patterns, screens, textures, and images printed on self-adhesive films. These are effective when used in combination with your own black line designs. In this example, begin with a sketch of your design. Have fun! Play around with it! This is the kind of designing where you can do a complete fantasy. Determine the size of your card and work within it to get a sketch you like.*

2. *Transfer your sketch to the paper on which you will do your finished art. Using a cork-backed metal or metal-edged ruler and a technical pen, ink in the linework using different pen points for variety. Correct mistakes with white opaque correction paint. Let it dry and then work on top of it. The key to success with inked linework is patience. Let one area dry before going on to the next; otherwise you'll only smear the ink and drive yourself crazy. As you ink, go back with a kneaded eraser and take out the linework you no longer need. Note that not all the areas are enclosed by black line. It's very important to keep this kind of design very clean; dirt or fingerprints trapped beneath the film is not removable.*

3. *Having completed the linework, begin laying in film. Be certain each area is clean. Lay down a piece of screened film over the area you want to cover. The piece should extend a little beyond the area. Using a cutting knife, delicately cut along the edges and carefully pull away the excess film. Rub the film down with a burnisher. Do this with great care. be sure not to rub the edges the wrong way. If you rub too hard, you risk tearing the film.*

4. *Put down all the other patterns in exactly the same way. This is an exciting medium to play with and it's easy! The possibilities are as limitless as your imagination. Look at the fun of this Sophisticated design and then try your own version of this technique with different kinds of subject matter.*

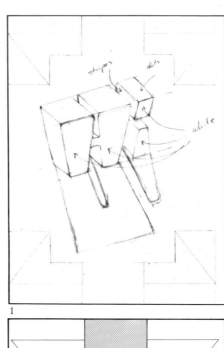

1

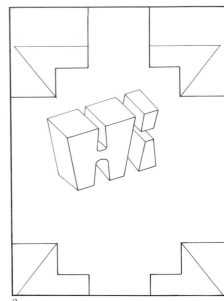

2

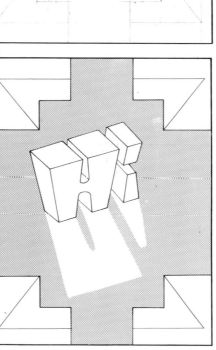

3

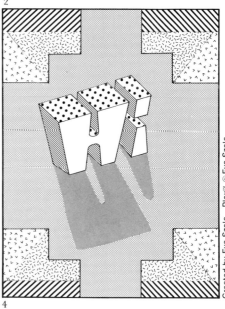

4

Created by Eva Szela Plex™ © Eva Szela

A dramatic and svelte example of a Sophisticated Blank Card. The elegance of the completely black cat against the light and delicate marguerites is striking and effective. Note that cats are among the very most popular subjects and can be counted on to be successful.

Whether you've selected one particular look that appeals to you or seems suited to your skills or whether you're still considering them as a whole, give some thought now to how gender affects the look and the potential success of each greeting card. This section is about how to make a card uniquely right for only women, only men, or both at the same time. There are some general qualities that will make a given card appropriate for each. It's important to keep in mind that these are guidelines, not hard and fast rules. Common sense should prevail whenever you feel something conflicts with the reality of what you are trying to create or accomplish.

Consider the possiblities for Masculine and Feminine looks inherent in the categories you examined in Chapter 1. With the exception of Sweetly Charming, which is decidedly and only Feminine, all other styles can be put together in ways that make them right for either gender or both at the same time.

The illustration shown right is an excellent example of the most general characteristics of a Feminine greeting card. The colors are mostly soft pastel shades. The images used are fluffy, billowy, or curly, soft, rounded, and light in feeling. Flowers are used. Not all these characteristics must be present for a card to have a distinctly Feminine feel, but you will find that invariably one or more of these characteristics will be present. Examine the illustration on page 39 again, only now in this context. Note that the design meets only a few of the criteria (soft pastel tones and light in feeling) and still it is distinctly Feminine in feeling.

The illustration of the big horn sheep, shown here, on the other hand, is a prime example of a Masculine design. The colors are rich, deep, dark, and include a lot of brown. The images are angular, hard, and heavy in feeling. Animals that can be readily associated with aggression or sport are used. Other symbols of various sports (golfing accessories, decoys, fishing equipment, and so on) are also appropriate.

IF WISHES WERE FLOWERS, ID PICK SOME FOR YOU, AND MAKE YOU A GARLAND OF WISHES COME TRUE.

©1986 BY PEGGY JO ACKLEY

❀ HAPPY BIRTHDAY ❀

In this excellent example of a Feminine greeting card the images used are fluffy, billowy, or curly, soft, rounded, and light. The colors are soft, pastel shades and pink is used. There are flowers. Only women and girls are depicted. Note the use of fragile, vining flowers enhances the sense of sweetness and lightness. The entire design has a feeling of delicacy.

Again, not all these elements must be present for a card to have a distinctly Masculine feeling, but when one or more is, you will generally find that card seems more appropriate for a man. Examine the illustration on page 43 again and note now that the character depicted on the cover has distinctly Masculine traits. That single element might prohibit a woman from sending that card to another woman, even though it is hilariously funny, because she might feel that neither of them was represented through the card. However, she would feel entirely comfortable sending it to a man and in that sense this card still succeeds.

Remember that these are broad guidelines. There are women with tailored tastes who abhor fluffy, cutesy *anything* and there are men who would plead to receive a greeting card with any color other than brown on it. If you know you want to appeal to one individual or a group of people whose tastes are other than the general, by all means go ahead and do so. The guidelines here are the very broadest followed by that portion of the field aiming to appeal to the greatest proportion of the population as a whole.

You may also appeal to neither gender directly or to both in one design by achieving a Neuter look, meaning the greeting card does not look decidedly Feminine or Masculine. The step-by-step demonstration on pages 24–25 shows the creation of a Thank You card with a Neuter look.

In reviewing this chapter you might keep in mind that there is no such thing as a right or wrong style. There is only what's right or not for you, and only *you* can determine that. If you feel that one style has captured your imagination and you find ideas popping up all over as you study it, take notes and save the ideas. When you're ready to tackle a design, review these notes. Trying more than one style is a good idea too. Sometimes you may surprise yourself with an aptitude you didn't know you had. It's also good to come back and reread this book as you work in any one area. Different things will begin to have greater meaning the more involved you become. What was a mystery to you yesterday will suddenly become clear tomorrow because

you've worked in that area for a while and now understand more. Always remember that these guidelines are just that; they are not hard and fast rules. The important thing to comprehend is *why* each suggestion was made. Knowing that frees you to begin to break the rules, but in smart ways. That will result in fun, new, exciting ideas for the greeting cards of tomorrow!

This Blank Card is an excellent example of the kind of ruggedness, weight, and dark color scheme that are typical of a design with specifically Masculine appeal.

3
CHOOSING
SUBJECTS
THAT APPEAL

HAVING examined the more common sending situations for greeting cards as well as some of the more popular styles of artwork, consider now the importance of the subject matter selected for use on your card. How would Aunt Tessie, who grows African violets and keeps cats, feel when she opens her birthday card and finds it's illustrated with a large buffalo on the open prairie? Fitting the subject matter to the occasion and to the recipient of the card is crucial. This chapter discusses the more commonly used subjects, with some thoughts about each.

FLORALS

Women like florals. Women send greeting cards. Those two facts make this a very important area for you to consider. Everything is a symbol of something. Flowers can be beautiful symbols of thoughtfulness, caring, and love. Two flowers are a lovely symbol of Friendship. Either one or two roses is a symbol of Romantic Love. Tiny flowers and buds are excellent for Baby. Lilies of the valley and other flowers are popular for Wedding. Lilies are right for Sympathy. These situations are not limited to those flowers. *All* kinds of flowers work well for Birthday and Anniversary. Mixing different kinds to create unique color feelings can be fun especially for Birthday. Bright, cheery flowers are terrific for Get Well. Blank cards are also a great opportunity for just about anything Floral, as shown in the following step-by-step demonstration.

The portrayal of a young girl on the beach is a pleasant and comfortable combination. Showing the girl from the back keeps her age unknown and increases the sendability of this blank card.

DEMONSTRATION SIX

DRAWING A

FLORAL CARD WITH

SHADED PENCIL

In this example the design is a rose, perhaps the most favorite greeting card subject matter. You can never have too many roses! The sending situation is friendship. There is no editorial on either the cover or the inside. Shaded pencil is a beautifully elegant and understated manner of working. The delicacy and sensitivity of the design is a compliment to anyone who receives it. A sense of quality is inherent in its look.

1. *Begin by sketching your design. When doing roses, always use the earlier stages of bloom to achieve an optimistic and positive feeling. Heavy-weight tracing vellum is excellent for this kind of work because the tooth is just right. If you've not worked in this medium before, you might begin with an HB lead in a mechanical pencil; it's neither too soft nor too hard.*

2. *An added benefit of tracing vellum is that it's excellent for making changes in your design. In this example, for instance, you like the rose and leaves, but don't care for the axis created by the stem. So you revise that relationship.*

3. *Position your design within the card area you've chosen. Begin to lightly shade the deepest areas. These are usually anything that is behind something else (like the petals of the rose) or, in the case of a curved surface, the part that is farthest away from you. As you shade in these areas, feather the gray lightly as you come away from them. If you do something you don't like, just press your kneaded eraser over it repeatedly and lift the lead out.*

4. *Continue in this way, remembering that you can lighten with your kneaded eraser and darken with your pencil as you choose. The end result is a lovely, delicate rose anyone would love to share with a friend.*

1

2

3

4

5. *If you prefer a looser look, be looser when you do Steps 2 and 3 and shade in only a few selected areas!*

Pay attention to the essential form of the kind of flower you select. Daisies are *very* popular. Select softer, more rounded shapes in general rather than spikey, pointed forms. There are always exceptions, of course. The bird of paradise, for example, is perceived by many to be a fashionable and elegant bloom, but to others it might be simply exotic and weird. You would probably position it as Sophisticated were you to illustrate it. However, if you want to achieve an American Country look, you would be well advised to look for a simpler and more innocent looking flower, such as a tulip, rose bud, or impatiens (see the illustrations on pages 41 and 45.)

Flowers can be beautifully illustrated in all the styles you've examined. Take a moment and go through the book looking at the illustrations again, this time with an eye just to the Florals. You will be amazed at how many different ways there are of using and styling flowers. It's an exciting and fun opportunity for you, especially if you like flowers. It's doubly rewarding if you grow them yourself because you'll be able to do the best possible research.

Daisies appeal to everybody. If they're not in your garden, you can always find them at a florist. The following step-by-step demonstration is an exciting example of designing perky daisies with pastels. Compare this Floral demonstration with the preceding one. Note the importance of the type of styling and the medium in creating very different effects.

Keep the season in mind when selecting a flower to illustrate. Some are so associated with specific seasons (poinsettia with Christmas; daffodil, crocus, lilac, and tulip with spring; carnation in fall colors with fall) that to use them elsewhere would be confusing. Seasonally specific flowers should only be used in sending situations that relate directly to the seasonal limitations each flower is perceived to have. For example, use daffodils on Easter cards and fall-colored carnations for Thanksgiving.

Pastel designs are often characterized by their spontaneity and verve. There is a freshness and energy inherent in pastel work that is definitely suited to Floral greeting cards. Unfortunately the relative fragility of pastel designs is a limitation.

In this example the subject matter is daisies done in a Stylized manner. Your sending situation will be Friendship, Thinking of You. The cover will say, "I've been thinking about you . . ." and the inside will say, ". . . and just wanted to let you know." Because pastels are opaque, you may use colored papers. Select a paper with an interesting texture since it will be an essential part of your design.

1

4

2

3

5

1. Keeping the subject matter in mind, consider the color possibilities. The white and yellow of the daisies and green of the leaves would be set off nicely by a fresh blue background. Gather some examples of different colored paper stock and try out pastel shades on them to get a feel for how to plan your design.

2. Determine the size of your greeting card. Make a mat by cutting that size area out of a larger piece of paper. Begin to sketch your daisies. Stay loose. Try several possibilities. Lay your mat over the sketches a number of different ways to explore layout possibilities. Decide which one you like best and develop that further.

3. As you are developing this sketch, do a rough layout of your lettering. Whether you plan to do your own or not it's always a good idea to consider it at this point because it will eventually be an integral part of your design.

6

7

8

4. Use the graphite transfer method described in the Appendix to transfer your sketch to the colored paper upon which you intend to do your finish. Beginning with the darker colors, fill in those areas you want dark. Keep your strokes simple. Remember you want to achieve a spontaneous look.

5. Work in the medium ranges. Take care that the direction of your strokes is appropriate to the area they're in. Avoid blending. It would interfere with the clean, simple look you're trying to achieve.

6. Come in now with the very lightest tones. Add them with dash! Add any additional dark tones for the fullest effect.

7. If you want to do the lettering on your original, transfer your rough and paint it in the color of your choosing. Do this with extreme care so as not to smear the very fragile pastels. A border seems like a good finishing touch, so add it.

8. Now place your mat over the design. This gives you a good idea of what your design will look like when it is cropped in an actual greeting card!

ANIMALS

Animals (including birds) also work well in every style you examined in Chapter 2. Animals are a popular subject for greeting cards. Animals done realistically or in a Stylized manner will work for a variety of situations. They are often good for Masculine and General looks. Endangered species and more exotic jungle, mountain, and plains animals are often used on the blank card format. Cats, birds, squirrels, mice, dogs, porcupines—really just about any North American animal that can be made to seem nonthreatening—can be styled as Sweetly Charming or Whimsical. They will all work as long as there is nothing unpleasant associated with them. In general, avoid predators or at the very least, predatory situations. Exaggerating their endearing qualities, like extra large ears and eyes on mice, and minimizing their unpleasant qualities, like less obtrusive tails on mice, is the key to styling any animal in the Sweetly Charming or Whimsical manner.

Almost every kind of animal is used in one way or another for Humorous cards. Do whatever you need to make it funny. Giving animals human characteristics, clothing, posture, or gestures is a technique that works.

When working with animals keep their seasonal context in mind. Ducks, chicks, and rabbits are all associated with Easter. When you use them in another context, you risk confusion. Watch also for gender

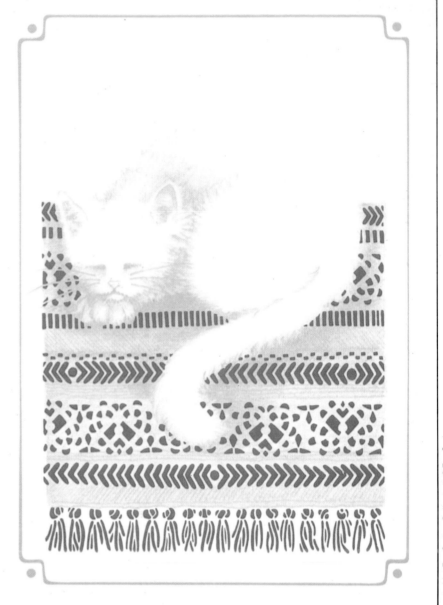

Created by Eva Szela   *Delicates*™ ©Eva Szela

Cats are extremely popular subject matter. This softly rendered sleeping cat is a handsome example of a good general use of the subject on a Blank Card.

identification. Bears (not teddies) usually look Masculine, for example. That's all right as long as you're using a bear in that specific context. If you want to illustrate a winter bird, do so, but perhaps not on a Birthday card, since you may limit the useful life of the design to only half the year. Apply that particular design to a Christmas card instead. As for gender identification, if you want to illustrate a lion, go ahead, but be aware that it looks very Masculine and apply it to a Father's Day card.

You can't go wrong with animals if you think of them always as symbols, either of the person sending the card or of the person receiving the card. Do whatever you feel will be in keeping with each particular sending situation you design. So if you want to do a Realistic animal and you want to do it for a Feminine Birthday card, select an animal that is already delicate and pretty, perhaps a domestic cat, and illustrate it in a Realistic, but graceful, way. Or if you want to do a Sweetly Charming Get Well card, select a perky animal, perhaps a bluebird, and exaggerate its endearing qualities, in this case its fluffiness, and illustrate it in a bright and cheerful way.

Whatever style you select and whatever animal you use will work for you if you keep the sending situation in mind and think of the animal as a symbol of either the sender or the recipient.

The natural charm of the winterbird and the richness of its surroundings are all good notes to hit when creating a traditional Realistic Christmas design.

May your holidays

be filled

with love and joy

PERSONAL PERSPECTIVE

JOHN C.W. CARROLL

"I've been creating greeting cards for ten years and am the Product Manager for Creative Papers by C. R. Gibson. Originally I came to the business inadvertently. The first greeting cards I made were *not* done for the card business, but to help promote a book I had published that worked well in nontraditional outlets; that is, it sold in gift shops as easily as it sold in book stores. Ultimately, the cards I made to promote the book, Richard Stine's *Smile in a Mad Dog's i,* went on to become my main project and I stopped publishing books.

Our trade is in tremendous flux right now, so I'm not sure how I feel about the industry as a whole. I certainly enjoy *what* we do: Our product is positive, helpful, utilitarian, expressive, supportive, and aids communication. However, gone are the "us" and "them" days, as we in the alternative side are less distinguishable from them, the majors, the established companies, in style and marketing approach. There is a part of me, indeed, that regrets having to get serious. I recognize, though, that we operate to be successful in business, and this goal requires growing sophistication.

There is a certain conceptual pleasure in being a successful business person and being an effective competitor. It is rewarding on that level. But I miss the thrill of being part of a new business, as we knew it in the late 1970s and early 1980s, for example, on the fourth floor of the Colisseum at the annual Stationery Show in New York City.

When I'm looking for designs for my own line, I try not to have preconceptions, so I remain receptive to every new idea that presents itself. However, I have definite ideas about what the line needs, and this guides my selection of artists. As to the artist, I look for self-starters, because I don't art-

direct. If I find a style that I like that is appropriate, and I can convey my needs as I develop the line, then I get out of the artist's way. I want to work with artists who can make it on their own, understanding my needs almost intuitively. In this sense, an artist who craves freedom is best for me, not an artist who requires that every detail be ordered and described. In the artist's work I mostly look for quality of execution and a sense of color, composition, and assurance, insofar as that can ever be seen.

When an artist is creating work for greeting cards the most important characteristic is sendability. It's never enough just to be great art. Ours is a product that is used, not just appreciated. I have not gotten comfortable yet with the whole category of deep, personal expression cards, but it seems to be a category vigorously pursued by many companies. I think they are a little too canned for my personal taste. Humor remains high on my list of interests. When you are considering the appropriateness of your own style of work, I think the key is knowing the company you're soliciting: It would be inappropriate to submit Sweetly Charming to Maine Line or gay humor to Blue Mountain. There will always be a need for pretty as well as for funny cards. Other stylistic considerations will come and go as a reflection of our society, a market segment, or regional tastes.

When addressing the sending situation, I always remind artists not to reinvent the symbology we associate with the occasions of our lives. An artist should include visual information to reinforce use/sendability. I tend also to focus Friendship images toward a specific Friendship message, such as "Miss you," "Please write," or "Thinking of you."

Birthdays, of course, seem endlessly fertile and can

become narrowly oriented if a company has enough outreach. Age-specific cards for Juveniles are an example, as are relative-specific cards.

There are also no hard and fast rules about imagery for cards. I published an image that was wrong in almost every regard—a bad photo of real people, nonoccasional, esoteric caption on front, and blank inside—yet it was my all-time best-seller for years and remains in the line at Carolyn Bean after eight years plus!

Greeting cards can be an attractive opportunity when added to an artist's on-going assignment mix. However, the satisfaction will depend on how the manufacturer buys— whether by the single image or by a collection—and how the illustrator works—is he or she capable of doing many styles effectively? Is it wise to work with many companies? Will any of those companies restrict whom else an artist works for? I always find there is something about the nature of the product that makes its creation satisfying. I feel the sort of freedom I offer the artist is an attraction in itself. I want an artist to be pleased with the work. If he or she is not happy, it comes out in the work. Then of course there is the palpable sense of gratification an artist can have when he or she finds the cards in the best local shops."

I LIKE YOU

DAILY NEWS

UFO SIGHTING

...YOU'RE STRANGE!

In this card published by C.R. Gibson the artist chose the strange-and-wonderful approach to the Humorous slam. Note the use of an anthropomorphized horse to enhance the charm and wit of the greeting card.

LANDSCAPES AND
INTERIORS

The key to making either landscapes or interiors into successful greeting cards is to put something in each one that will symbolize the emotional intent of the greeting card. Light is one way to do this. A sunrise or sunset in a landscape, lamplight, or sunlight streaming in a window will immediately flood the setting with emotion. You can also add significant objects: In a landscape add a rainbow for hope or cheer; sheep, a barn, or house for hominess and tranquility; flowers for Femininity; in an interior a cat or vase of flowers for Femininity; a reading lamp or chair (or both) for hominess; two coffee cups for Friendship. Both landscapes and interiors can be done in any style and will work very well for any sending situation as long as the elements are in keeping with things characteristic of that situation.

A birthday is a perfect time for dreaming brand new dreams!

This delightful Whimsical Birthday goose is the focal point of a lakeside landscape. This is a good use of the landscape on a greeting card.

Wishing you
new dreams come true!

PEOPLE

Care should be taken when illustrating people for greeting cards, especially when done in a Realistic manner. You now know how important it is for your card to work in as many ways as possible within its sending situation. Realistically styled people, like any other subject matter, are the symbols of either the sender or the recipient of the card. The physical characteristics of each person depicted become restrictions in terms of who can send the card to whom. For instance, if both you and your friend are overweight and you have brown hair and your friend has blond hair, are you going to feel good about sending her a Birthday card with an illustration of a svelte blond holding a bouquet of flowers? Sending such a card could actually be seen as an insult if your friend is sensitive. By using a person Realistically on your card you may inadvertently restrict its sendability. It's best when doing people Realistically to obscure specific features. An example of this is shown in the illustration on page 17.

Illustrating people in other manners (Sweetly Charming, Whimsical, Humorous, Stylized) is less risky. You will necessarily *have* to exaggerate or caricature the person illustrated and in doing so will generalize him or her.

Pay attention to gender identification. Ascertain whether a man or a woman is appropriate for a given situation and be sure that your illustration communicates the gender that you've judged to be right.

Birthdays build character.

Created by Eva Szela   Lizbess™ ©Eva Szela

This Whimsical design uses a highly stylized woman as its focal point. It is unusual to combine whimsey and humor in this way.

Believe it!

The task of examining every possible object you might choose with which to illustrate your greeting card would be as immense as examining every word in the dictionary. The reality is that you can put absolutely anything on a greeting card. Just remember a few basic points about what a greeting card is when making your choices: A card is usually sent by a woman; it should make the recipient feel good; its subject is a symbol for either the sender or the receiver of the card or the emotion the card expresses.

Some effective symbols for specific sending situations are examined in Chapter 1. Some additional ones are used again and again because of their consistent success.

Teddy bears are one of the most popular subjects around. They work in any style; they're right for women, men, and children. You almost can't go wrong with teddy bears. They represent nostalgia for adults and the real world for children. They symbolize warmth, security, coziness, affection, sweetness, and sometimes Masculinity. The teddy bear does a lot of work on greeting cards. Be aware that the very popularity of this subject means that there is a lot of competition out there that already has the teddy bear working for it. Your challenge then is to come up with a fresh, new, fun version of your own using this tried-and-true subject.

Seashells have always been and continue to be one of the most popular design motifs used for greeting cards. This Blank Card features a lovely illustration of shells.

The heart shape is an excellent symbol and is used often. It works in any styling except Realistic. It can communicate Friendship, Romantic Love, sexuality, or familial love—depending on the context in which it's used. Any editorial in conjunction with this symbol will affect its interpretation.

The star is another excellent symbol. It can be done in any manner and symbolizes importance, excitement, nighttime, romance, or inspiration depending on the context in which it's used. Here too editorial will have terrific impact on how this symbol is interpreted.

The welcome wreath, large brimmed hats, and the welcome pineapple are all strong Country symbols.

The butterfly symbolizes femininity and beauty.

Confetti and streamers have come into recent use as symbols of celebration. They are effective on their own and they are also exciting when used in conjunction with other symbols. Combine them with a Birthday celebration. Do them in combination with a red rose and suddenly Anniversary is festive; with a bouquet of flowers, Feminine is bright and lively. The possibilities are limitless here.

It's challenging and fun to come up with your own new objects. They should work as symbols of positive and upbeat things. Whatever subject matter you choose to illustrate your greeting card, if you keep the basic charactcristics of a successful card in mind, you're going to create a highly successful card! Have fun with it and give your imagination full rein!

The teddy bear is very popular subject matter. This Whimsical styling shows the use of a teddy as a Valentine motif. This subject can be used in almost any sending situation as long as it is adapted and made appropriate by the use of support elements like the hearts and editorial on this card.

God is not the only one who loves you!

Happy Valentine's Day

"And now these three remain: faith, hope and love. But the greatest of these is love." I CORINTHIANS 13:13 NIV

4
CREATING CARDS FOR HOLIDAYS

Santa Claus is such a very appealing subject that it will work in an extremely broad spectrum of sending situations. Note that in addition to the use of very traditional subject matter this design also makes ample use of red and green. The rich detail and immense charm of this Stylized design can only enhance the positive impact of this Christmas classic.

THIS chapter will explore many of the sending situations created by holidays occurring throughout the year. As you saw in Chapter 1, any card that is not written and/or designed with a specific holiday motif or reference is an Everyday card. So every card that is written and/or designed using a specific holiday motif or reference is a Seasonal card.

This chapter will outline some of the major seasons and explore those characteristics that make a greeting card appropriate for each one. Not all holidays will be included, just the ones that address the needs of very large market segments. Certain holidays may be more or less of interest to you.

Subject matter, style, and editorial all combine to make each card right for a particular holiday. That basic principle will remain the same from one holiday to another; only the specifics will change.

Begin by picking subject matter that is related to the actual, literal,

physical celebration of the holiday. Determine colors that are generally perceived to be characteristic of either the holiday itself or the season of the year when the holiday occurs. Use or write editorial that makes specific reference to words, concepts, or phrases commonly used in celebration of the holiday. Then design your greeting card in whatever style you choose (as outlined in Chapter 2) combining as many of these elements as possible.

Seasonal greeting cards are a whole separate area of opportunity for which to exchange cards. The challenge for you will be to understand what makes a good one good and then go on to create something you feel is even more delightful, inspirational, celebratory, or fun for whichever season or seasons appeal to you.

Christmas is far and away the most popular of all the seasons. In some parts of commercial greeting cards, there is as much volume in Christmas cards as there is in all the Everyday cards combined.

For many people, Christmas cards are a predominant means of keeping in touch. In these days of hectic pace and stress-ridden careers, friends separated by distance are sometimes only in contact through Christmas cards. Indeed, for many, the most comprehensive guide to who's who and what's what in various relationships is their ever-cherished Christmas card list. However you explain the phenomenon, it's a rare person who doesn't rather automatically send out some kind of mailing during these holidays. That explains the importance and magnitude of this particular category of Seasonal cards.

When one is buying and/or designing one's Christmas cards, the design and editorial need to be appropriate for sending to a wide range of friends, relatives, acquaintances, and business associates. This is important to keep in mind when creating these cards. Since the holidays are a busy time for everyone, one often tries to fulfill all of one's Christmas card needs with one or two boxes of cards. Thus the necessity for each design and piece of writing to be appropriate for a number of different relationships. That is one of the great challenges of creating Christmas cards.

An important element to consider when creating your Christmas design is the subject matter. There are many, many choices here for topics steeped in tradition. As you examine various subjects, keep in mind the color factor. Almost *always* use a lot of red and/or green. This is one rule that it's risky to depart from. Sometimes blue is used and it will work, as will other colors, but then you should be certain you are at least using traditional subject matter. Be aware that you are departing from the tried and true in the context of a holiday that is intrinsically all about tradition.

If you are doing the writing yourself, remember that each card must be right for a number of different sending situations and so the message must be general. You can't beat "Season's Greetings" and "Happy Holidays" for generality. Even "Merry Christmas" is less general than the other two because it can

Nostalgic subject matter works so well for Christmas cards. This Realistic styling of a charming country church takes one back to the memory of (or the sentimental wish for) the muffled silence of freshly fallen snow on Christmas eve. The lighted windows are warm and inviting, making one think of community and love.

May joy and peace
be yours
throughout the holiday season
and New Year

only be sent to a Christian; there may be many people on Christmas card lists to whom even this seemingly broad message will not apply.

Good Christmas subject matter is anything that instills a positive feeling about the occasion, anything that says Christmas. These are usually images recalling a nostalgic or perhaps ideal Christmas. For some this might be a little country church in the snow or an imaginative Santa Claus laden with a heavy sack of Christmas gifts. For others it could be the gleam of diffused wintry sunshine glowing on clean snow that recalls the memory of crisp, clear icy cold Christmas days. Consider the sheer festivity of the season, the music. Anything having to do with music will work: sheet music, musical instruments, choirs or choirboys, bells, or trumpets. A wonderful Christmas tree is always popular as in the illustration opposite.

Religious and inspirational aspects of Christmas are of great importance to many people. There is always a demand for designs depicting the nativity scene, Mary and Joseph on their journey, the three wise men, and anything related to the event of that momentous evening. The star of Bethlehem is also a good symbol. Maybe you can combine it with a general winter scene to create an inspirational Christmas design.

For others Christmas means the traditions associated with its celebration (Christmas cards, of course, being one of them). Cookies, fruitcakes, candy canes, gifts, stockings hung for Santa to fill. Santa is one of the most important images associated with Christmas and an excellent one to use on a greeting card. The illustration shown on page 77 is an example of using Santa on a Humorous poster sent as a Christmas card. Also remember to take advantage of Santa-related material; reindeer are popular and so are Santa's elves.

Any of the images suggested in "The Twelve Days of Christmas" or *'Twas the Night Before Christmas* is apt. The partridge in the pear tree is a particularly popular selection from the former. Mistletoe is another strong tradition, as is the welcome wreath on the door. The illustration on page 76 is a charming combination of just such a wreath and a

Hope the best gifts this season are the joys of the heart.

This yellow background works nicely with the reds and greens to add warmth and hominess to this strong Christmas subject matter: the Christmas tree. And you can never go wrong with a teddy bear. The shape of the tree is idealized and the ornaments are charming. The Whimsical styling is perfect for the subject matter. The editorial skillfully ties in the gifts under the tree while, at the same time, minimizing the potentially commercial context of the packages.

Country goose, also a great subject matter for this season.

Some additional Christmas classics are the dove, a symbol of peace; candles, an inspirational approach; angels, a charming example of which is the illustration shown far right. Redbirds, such as cardinals, provide ideal opportunities to work in the all-important Christmas red and are good traditional subjects as well. A delightful example of cardinals is in the illustration shown on page 78. The poinsettia is the flower most strongly associated with Christmas. Don't overlook the potential of almost any other flower (certainly the rose) used either in combination with holly and/or pine or with red and green items of some sort. For that matter, don't overlook both holly and pine as subjects in themselves.

Things associated with winter will also work, like a winter bird or a snowman as in the illustration shown on page 78. The winter village also has a nostalgic association and can be designed in a charming way.

The most general, all-purpose approach to a Christmas card design that can be all things to all people is a card that is predominantly editorial, designed with lettering as the focal point, with other understated elements complementing the whole. The illustration shown on page 79 is an excellent example, although the editorial isn't completely predominant here.

As with all the examples shown throughout the book, these are intended to inspire you by breadth of possibility in not only subject matter but style and technique. Study each one and take from them those aspects and elements that interest you, that seem pertinent to you and your way of working. Remember that these are not the only right ways of doing Christmas designs. These are the ways that these designers, artists, and writers have chosen to do *their* designs. Yours should be entirely your own and completely different — completely you!

Joyous Holiday Greetings

The coziness and warmth implicit in the Country styling of this card are well suited to a successful Christmas card. This example shows an excellent use of a Christmas wreath based on the highly popular Everyday welcome wreath. The addition of a charming Country goose makes this one a sure winner. Note how positive and yet still very general the editorial is.

This example of a Christmas angel is very charming. The delightful whimsey of the situation gives this Christmas card a lovely touch. The star border highlights the spirituality of this Whimsical styling.

WARMTH AND LOVE
TO YOU AT CHRISTMAS

This humorous use of Santa is original and exciting in that it is a 25″ × 35″ poster sent as a Christmas "card." Traditional reds and greens abound. Santa himself is depicted in very non-traditional ways and in such a manner that there's a Santa for virtually everyone.

Cardinals are a very traditional subject. Here the wonderful use of red and delightful animation bring this Whimsical Christmas card to life. The spirit of the season is skillfully communicated, while the copy is upbeat and very general.

Fa-la-la-la-la....!

Created by Eva Szela   Snookie the Snowperson™ ©Eva Szela

WISHING YOU ALL THE JOY

AND MERRINESS

OF A HAPPY HOLIDAY SEASON!

(Left)
The snowman is a Christmas classic. This design uses a lot of red and green in keeping with the holiday and also incorporates other bright colors for a fun, positive feeling. The tiny red cardinals add a note of lightness.

JOYOUS GREETINGS AND BEST WISHES

FOR THE NEW YEAR

(Right)
The lettering of the word "PEACE" is a very predominant part of this very beautiful and highly successful Christmas design. The design itself and its colors are rich and muted. The feeling evoked is one of spirituality and caring.

"My entry into the world of greeting cards was an indirect one. I graduated from the Rhode Island School of Design with a degree in sculpture. I had planned, rather idealistically, for a life in the fine arts, but unexpected twists and turns in life's path led to a ten-year career as a designer with a large Midwest greeting card corporation which is a leader in the social expression industry. The time I spent there provided me with professional experience in creating and designing a wide range of products, including greeting cards, giftwrap, calendars, and albums, and I gathered valuable background and experience in the industry. I had the opportunity to explore and develop different styles and techniques and to familiarize myself with the many technical processes that can be effectively used in the design and production of greeting cards. And of course, this gave me the security of a good salary and benefits. However, I experienced a deep inner discomfort with the corporate lifestyle and the limits that it imposed on my creative freedom, and hence growth and happiness.

Recognizing these things to be of far greater value to me than the security offered, I left the job and moved to the quiet and beauty of rural Vermont, where I found a place well out of the mainstream that nourished me and my work. Here I began a new career as a freelance designer/illustrator. Fortunately, my background and experience, plus a portfolio of printed samples, served me well as I began to make contact with greeting card companies throughout the country. I was delighted and relieved when my work was desired by clients right away. A handful of these early contacts have developed into very mutually satisfying professional relationships, conducted almost exclusively over the phone and through the mails. Clients consistently provide me with enough work to maintain a reasonable income and with enough creative freedom and affirmation so that I have been able to seek new design challenges and personal creative growth as I experience real development in my work.

My love for sculptural form and space carries into my two-dimensional designing and painting, and I work in a variety of styles and techniques. This enables me to do work for a number of clients and to provide each with a special look rather than to glut the marketplace with one recognizable style. I design for both Seasonal and Everyday lines. Some designs require, at the client's request, consideration of caption placement and a visual tie-in with the caption and inside sentiment. Other designs do not have a caption and are marketed by the client on the strength of the visual image alone, with perhaps an inside greeting added later. I enjoy working both ways, always keeping in mind the sending situation and the relationship between the sender and the recipient. I think it's very important to capture the implied warmth of this relationship in the design elements, layout, and color feeling of the card.

My approach is usually to use simple, uncluttered compositions with a very direct perspective on one or two important elements. For example, the amaryllis is presented so that it clearly extends its greeting to the recipient (see the illustration shown here). Flowers and animals evoke feelings of warmth and I use them frequently in my work. But relationships can also be suggested using inanimate objects, and a feeling of warmth can be captured through the use of color.

As I begin to work on a new design, I consider first the client and the sending situation. For an Everyday Birthday design, for example, I determine whether the client has indicated a need for a design with a specifically Masculine or Feminine feeling, and consider whether the client's market is conservative, traditional, or sophisticated. If a caption is provided (I do not do editorial copy), I must allow space within the design area and relate the design both to that space and to the mood or content of the copy.

When I begin to sketch, I always work within the perimeters of a template the size of the card, although this template is usually enlarged proportionally for my own comfort. It is important to begin working within the given dimensions, rather than try to make a design fit later. In the process of actually sketching the layout, subject ideas and design relationships begin to emerge and find places within the rough, which I work and rework until I am satisfied with it. I then send the sketch to the art director with notes to assist in visualizing the finished work, indicating how I plan to treat the painted finish, proposed color feeling, and the process suggestions, if relevant. There are instances when I'm able to take a design directly to the finish and then send it, and this is a great pleasure, but an exception. When the sketch is approved and returned I then transfer the design to the paper upon which I'll do my finish and paint it, always keeping in mind the importance of a warm color feeling. I usually work on many designs, painting the finish of one while another sketch is in the mail. There is a constant flow of artwork coming and going from my studio.

With this necessary volume of work, I find I must be a virtual wellspring of ideas and am amazed that I am constantly replenished. Essentially, the challenge for me seems to be to find new ways to present familiar images. Christmas is a good example, for our traditional Christmas symbols and colors remain the same year after year, and they are symbols that the consumer is generally most comfortable with. An exception to this is my Christmas amaryllis, designed to appeal to a very Sophisticated market.

I incorporate traditional symbols in a design and make them appear fresh and new through innovative layouts, decorative borders, patterned backgrounds, and other styling techniques. Many ideas germinate while I keep an eye on current design trends, as well as review visual histories of art and design. But the final inspiration always comes from within. I try to bring good information (product knowledge and design research) to the creative process, but once the process starts and I begin sketching, I let my intuition take over, staying open to new ideas and directions as they emerge on the paper. Through this process I've found much joy in my work and have grown to know myself better— wonderful side benefits to earning a living!

The simplicity of my layouts reflect the serenity and balance that I seek in my own life and that many others recognize and share. I have learned that my best work comes from the heart, from the intuitive part of the process, and perhaps that is what others feel as well.

I love to work, and my designs are finished to a degree that reflects the caring and attention I put into them. I am grateful that designing greeting cards enables me to put my work into the marketplace where it is available to so many people, hopefully bringing them warmth and delight and a means of sharing these feelings with others. **99**

Holiday Greetings

This formal Floral Christmas card by Stephanie Stouffer relies on an elegant amaryllis plant framed by a series of equally elegant borders to create a Sophisticated card. While the amaryllis traditionally blooms around the Christmas season, it is not usually portrayed on Greeting cards, thus creating an appealing newness to this design.

VALENTINE'S DAY

Valentine's Day is predominantly for lovers but not exclusively so. Friends also exchange Valentine's Day cards as do children. Sending these greeting cards is a relatively popular practice at this time, though not as extensive as Christmas, of course. Whether it's Romantic or the more universal kind, love is definitely the theme for Valentine's Day. Anything that symbolizes love is appropriate subject matter. Lace and ribbons are very good here. Cupids are traditional. The red rose is the prime symbol of love. Red and/or pink are the colors characterizing this holiday. The illustration shown here is an excellent example of a classic Valentine. The heart is an all-important motif. But hearts can also be a secondary element to support, say, an ever-popular teddy bear on a more general, universal love kind of Valentine. The illustration shown on the opposite page on the other hand is a Sophisticated and dynamic design, definitely Romantic and aimed squarely at the younger individual. A step-by-step demonstration of it follows. Valentine's Day is a great opportunity for humor. Insult humor does especially well for this holiday. See Chapter 5 for additional points on Humorous and Valentine's Day.

The pinks and reds and the ornate and delicate complexity of this intricate, flowery design all combine to make this illustration a Valentine classic. The doves, ribbon, and hearts are all just right for the season and the use of the words "TRUE LOVE" is the perfect finishing touch.

This Sophisticated styling of the traditional heart motif uses reds and pinks predominantly to create a dynamic Valentine design that's just right for the younger sender and recipient.

Created by Eva Szela   Love Stuff™ © Eva Szela

HANUKKAH

The Hanukkah sending situation is growing in popularity. There is a far greater variety of greeting cards available today than ever before for Jewish consumers and friends. When designing for Hanukkah, use subject matter that is synonymous with the occasion. The most popular is the menorah. Also popular are the dreidel and the Star of David. The editorial should always make some reference to Hanukkah. Any styling is appropriate. All colors are used, but blue is the more popular.

I LOVE YOU . . .

A LOT.

Wax or oil crayons are amazingly fun to work with. Their colors are lovely, bright, and clear, especially appropriate when your sending situation is Valentine's Day. The cover has no copy and the inside says, "I love you . . . a lot." The styling is Sophisticated.

1. *Hearts are the prime subject for Valentine's Day. Begin by sketching your design.*

2. *Transfer your sketch to the paper upon which you'll do your finish. Since pink and red are the predominant Valentine colors, do this design on bright pink stock. Using a kneaded eraser, pick up as much of the transferred heart drawings as you can, leaving just enough of an impression to follow when completing the design. Working at a consistent angle, go in and apply quick, small diagonal strokes of background color.*

3. *With a deep rose go in and outline the largest hearts. Fill them in loosely using strokes that are on the same diagonal as those in the background.*

4. *With additional bright colors and the same diagonal strokes, do the smaller hearts. Back both the yellow and orange with white crayon. Add random tiny gray hearts as well as black outlined hearts for contrast. Also include some orange ones without white backing.*

1

2

3

4

5

6

7

5. *Using a small brush and either mineral spirits or turpentine, dilute the color on the surface of each heart and drag a few diagonal lines through each one. Always keep the diagonals consistent with those in the background. With about a ½" wide flat brush on the same diagonal, go through the entire design with either mineral spirits or turpentine. Sweep the colors slightly out of their current shapes. Your paper will be saturated with fluid. Allow it to dry thoroughly before proceeding. (A portable hair-*

dryer is a great boost to this process.)

6. *Add a red squiggle to the center of each pink heart. Define one side of each pink heart with a red line. Recolor the orange hearts and add more orange accents in the background for brightness.*

7. *Add a pink line around all the pink hearts. With the white crayon, add a reflection curve to each heart. Blend each one of these a little using your small brush and diluter. Now you're finished!*

The rich woodsy colors of this spring basket of tulips brings the showers and freshness of the season to mind. Because of the seasonality of the flowers this design will work very well for Easter. Its sendability is even broader, however, because the card has no editorial at all to limit its use.

EASTER

Easter is primarily a Religious holiday. Greeting cards are sent, but it's not a large occasion for card sending. If you choose to design a Religious aspect of Easter, you may want to review the Religious section in Chapter 1. The cross is a very strong symbol, particularly here.

If, on the other hand, you choose to explore the Easter Bunny side of this holiday, then Sweetly Charming and Whimsical stylings would be just right. The range of subject matter possibilities spans bunnies, chicks, and ducklings as well as Easter baskets, decorated eggs, and chocolate bunnies. Recommended colors are pastels. Yellow and lavender are virtually synonymous with Easter.

You can approach this holiday purely from the seasonal direction as well. Any spring flower such as the tulips shown here, crocuses, daffodils, and dogwood, is highly appropriate. The editorial should make mention of the holiday in any of the above contexts.

MOTHER'S DAY

Just about everyone has a mother. Just about everyone has strong feelings about her. Mother's Day cards are very popular. The kind of designing that's right for Mother's Day is very broad. Everything that is appropriate for women in general is right for Mother's Day when either the holiday or the mom is mentioned in the editorial. For example, the cover of the card might say, "A Mother Is Love," and the inside might say, "And yours has always been just right. Happy Mother's Day." Review Chapters 1–3 with an eye to Feminine images. In particular, remember florals, any and all kinds, are always highly appropriate for this special occasion.

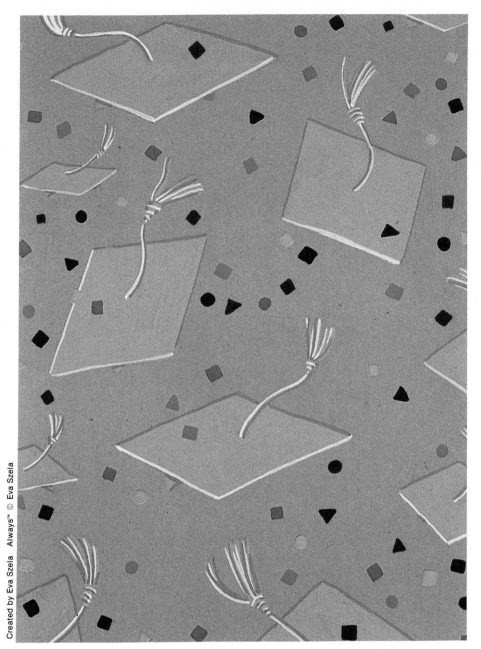

Created by Eva Szela   Always™ © Eva Szela

This is an excellent example of a festive Graduation design. The caps are thrown up in celebration and the mood is heightened by the addition of confetti.

WHAT AN ACHIEVEMENT!

CONGRATULATIONS GRADUATE!

Poor dad doesn't get remembered quite so often as mom, but cards are sent for Father's Day. Designing for this holiday means using Masculine elements and editorials that make specific references either to Father's Day or to Dad. You may want to review the section at the end of Chapter 2 about Masculine looks. There is ample opportunity for Humorous here as well. See Chapter 5 for more on this.

There are other holidays throughout the year. The ones discussed here are those for which the preponderant amount of card sending occurs. Graduation deserves some attention. Even though it's not literally a holiday, it's included as a Seasonal occasion. Typical graduation designs include cap and gown motifs, diplomas, ivy and inspirational scenes to urge the graduate onward and upward, as well as anything bookish. The editorial should make reference to the importance of the occasion. See the illustration of mortarboards shown opposite, for an example of Graduation design. (See a step-by-step demonstration of this card on pages 50 and 51.)

St. Patrick's Day is also an occasion for some card sending. The key to success here is a heavy use of green. Shamrocks, leprechauns, Irish landscapes, and St. Patrick himself are all popular images. The editorial can range from inspirational (mentioning the occasion, "the wearing of the green," or Irishness) to Humorous.

Seasonal designing is a fun and challenging addition to Everyday opportunities. If you feel a special affinity to a particular holiday, by all means take a run at that one. Your enthusiasm will probably communicate itself through your design and everyone will benefit!

DO ME A FAVOR

HADLEY ROBERTSON

5
CREATING HUMOROUS CARDS

TELL ME I'M ONE OF
THE BEAUTIFUL PEOPLE

This Humorous greeting card uses the Slam device. But since it is turned around and directed against the sender, its impact is softened considerably, possibly increasing its sendability.

THERE has been a lot of growth and excitement in the area of Humorous greeting cards recently. Fifteen or twenty years ago, greeting cards that were unlike the vast majority of those then available began to appear. Previously greeting cards *were only* fuzzy bunnies, red roses, and photographs of setting suns with formal captions on their covers like "To My Loving Aunt With Best Wishes" and rhymed verses inside. These kinds of cards are still available today because some people want them. But other people also want something else, and the huge greeting card companies weren't providing it.

What exactly "it" was varies from person to person and company to company, but everyone pretty much agrees on what "it" was and is: Alternative cards. Alternative cards are anything that is perceived to be unlike the traditional greeting card. That's why they are called "Alternative." They give the consumer a choice. This can mean something as

simple and obvious as providing an editorial that is straightforward, resembling conversation. It can mean a design that is simple, understated, a little rough, less presumptuous, less slick, sometimes actually crude and, therefore, warmer and more accessible to the people who buy, send, and receive cards. It can mean humor that is more adventuresome and more pertinent to life as it *really* is than on traditional studio cards, which are often fraught with visual and editorial clichés. However, clichés survive for a reason. They still live and thrive in some areas because there are people who still want them.

Alternative, to many, is something, anything that seems more real. It speaks to real issues, situations, people. Today they have come to be viewed as almost exclusively Humorous. This chapter explores some of the basic precepts of creating Humorous greeting cards. These apply to *all* kinds of humor. The examples shown will be drawn almost entirely from Alternative greeting cards since that's where it's happening.

The popularity of Humorous greeting cards today is astounding. It's an important area and one that warrants your attention. Give it some thought, even if you've never considered the possibility of creating these kind of cards before. The range of style is limitless and new ones are popping up all the time. You can really get creative and have some fun.

Humor is a way for people to send greeting cards that don't really say anything personal. Yet that person does say, in a very indirect and light way, "I care about you, but I'm not really saying so out loud. You can tell by the fact that I sent you this funny card." It's an interesting phenomenon. There is intimacy in it, but it's very indirect. The terrific news is that this results in a lot of nonoccasion greeting card sending. A lot of these cards are sent just because the joke is funny and the person wants to share it. This sending takes place in addition to the normal Birthday and Friendship sending situations, so it results in a lot of volume.

All the sending situations outlined in Chapter 1 are right for Humorous except Sympathy. All the Seasonal situations outlined in Chapter 4 are also right for Humorous. These even include Religious cards (which may surprise some).

The most frequent subject matter is either people stylized in extreme ways that make them funny and charming or animals that are anthropomorphized. This means the animal is made funny by the addition of humanizing clothing, attitudes, postures, or situations. There are no rules in these stylings except to make it funny. Keep an eye on gender identification. Be aware of whether your image is Masculine, Feminine, or Neuter and how you *want* it to look.

Humor is extremely tricky to do. It's very subjective. What is hilarious to one person may be only mildly amusing to another. Yet it's fun to do funny. Don't decide that you can't do it without trying. Take a run at it; then take another. Nothing comes easily (or perhaps *few* things come easily) so keep trying, lighten up, go easy on yourself. Let your work rest for a while and go back to it later. Even if you do succeed and you're feeling great confidence in what you've achieved, come back at various intervals and review what you've done. Study the Humorous devices outlined in this chapter. Come back again and again. As your skills develop, thoughts and points raised will become more and more meaningful to you. Sometimes this can simply affirm a discovery you've just made. This affirmation can be of tremendous help in keeping you going in a direction of strength. As your level of expertise increases, you may find that things you felt were not possible at first become possible (or interesting) at a later date.

The devices that follow are general guidelines to creating Humorous designs and editorials. Either element can drive the Humorous card, or come first. The joke can be completely visual, that is, it's contained entirely in the illustration; or it can be entirely editorial with no image to support it. Or it can be a combination of an image and an editorial. Remember also there are different degrees of funny, from hilarious to simply light-handed, and they're all right depending on your specific needs.

There is also, sad to say, funny and *not funny*. When creating your ideas try them out on several people in the earliest stages. Try to find people who aren't going to worry about hurting your feelings and avoid people who might want to hurt your feelings. *Look at your jokes objectively!* Study their understandability. If you have to explain it, it doesn't work. Sorry. Whatever you do, don't get mad at the person who told you he or she didn't get it. That's not going to fix your joke and it could lose you a valuable critic (and perhaps friend). Face facts. Go back and work on it some more. Make either the image or the editorial clearer, simpler, whatever it takes. If it's a bad joke (it happens), throw it away. There are other jokes in you! Eventually you will become your own best critic. You've *got* to be honest with yourself, though. At the same time, you've got to go easy on yourself. Allow yourself to make mistakes, everyone does. Remember if you really *want* to do it, you *can* do it!

INSULT OR SLAM

Humorous greeting cards often rely on either an Insult or a Slam depending on how hard-hitting each one is. An example of an Insult is "With a face like yours" on the cover and "It's no wonder you never know which end is up" on the inside. The Insult is one of the most popular forms of humor in Humorous greeting cards today and, indeed, historically as well. But the more insulting the joke, the closer the relationship must be between sender and recipient. These cards are not (generally) sent as true hostile insults, but more as sarcastic exchanges, barbs between friends and loved ones.

To broaden the appeal of your Insult, you can soften it to a Slam, an example of which is shown right. Another use of the Slam is to turn it around and direct it back on the sender as in the illustration of the woman, shown on page 88. Yet another approach that works *very* well within this category, but which must be used in conjunction with the Birthday sending situation is the age-related Slam. The Insult or Slam will involve the advanced age of the person having the birthday. See the illustration shown on page 92 for a good example of this approach. Anything built around the strange-and-wonderful concept also works well. The idea is something like "Ours is a strange and wonderful relationship" on the cover and "You're strange and I'm wonderful" on the inside.

Created by Eva Szela Only Kidding™ © Eva Szela

This example of a Humorous greeting card was created using the Slam device. It's bright and Graphic and appeals to both men and women.

Keep your chins up!

Slams can also be directed against groups, an example of which is in the illustration shown on page 93. One of the most popular, most successful versions of this kind of Slam is women making fun of men as a group. Women love to do this. Extensive research and the continuing commercial success of these kinds of cards attest to this fact. This sort of card works well in general Friendship sending situations among women and is thus right in the thick of the prime market. The degree of hardness of the Slam varies, of course, but remember that the members of the group being slammed are *not* the potential recipients of these cards and so you can go a little harder and still be very general in your appeal. The illustration of the juggler, shown on page 94, for example, is relatively hardhitting, while another example of a woman, also on page 94, is a little softer in its language. An excellent example of a Humorous card that ridicules a certain type of man is shown on page 95.

This approach is perceived to be essentially sexual in its appeal even though it's intended as an exchange between women. This is because the topic is sexual in its general context to women. However, the relationship between the person receiving the card and the person sending the card is friendship, not sexual.

Examine the entire area of Humorous cards carefully. It's an important one today, because it's receiving a lot of attention and experiencing a lot of activity. It's a rapidly changing area as well. Be sure to get into the marketplace and study the work currently being published. Try to do this at least three or four times a year. Every two months is really best if you can manage it.

**You're the one over the hill.
Happy Birthday!**

The bright colors and delightful animation of this design make it right for sending and receiving by both women and men. This is an excellent example of a very popular device used in the creation of Humorous Birthday cards—the age Slam or Insult.

IT'S TIME
TO COME OUT OF THE CLOSET. . .

. . . AND ADMIT TO YUPPINESS!

This is an example of the Slam device being used against an entire group. It's executed in a bright, Graphic style making it appropriate for both men and women.

This example uses the Slam device to create *Humor directed at men in general. Note the use of a specifically Feminine character, a good idea when you know for certain that your audience is women.*

IT'S WHOSE BALLS THEY ARE

THAT REALLY COUNTS!

Relax!
It's not so much how many balls
you can keep in the air at one time . . . .

This illustration is an excellent example of using the Slam against men to create a Humorous greeting card. The card is intended for exchange between women. The styling is very Sophisticated and witty in itself.

AND THEY'RE A LOT NEATER

IN THEIR BOXES.

CATS ARE AN EXCELLENT
REPLACEMENT FOR MEN.
THEY'RE DEMANDING.
THEY SHED.
THEY PURR IF YOU RUB
THEIR TUMMIES.
THEY LIKE TO RUB AGAINST
YOUR LEGS.

MR. INDECISION

(Scientific name: homo frustratus.)

Hobby: Not sure.

Fav Color: A yellowish red, no... a greenish orange. No...

Fav Book: There's so many.

Fav T.V. Program: ditto.

Fav Sport: Individual or team?

Fav Sexual Position: Number 45. Let's see, maybe number 81, No, it's number 137! Yep. Definitely, maybe...

Best Date Ever Had: That's easy. It was Curtain #3. Or was that the electrician from Maine? No. I know. It was Curtain #1! That's it! Yeah. Hmmm. On the other hand, it could have been Box #2.

This illustration is a good example of woman-to-woman humor: the Slam against men as a group. Note the Memphis look; the Sophisticated styling is combined with soft, feminine colors on this Blank Card.

Created by Eva Szela   Men: Legends in Their Own Minds™   © Eva Szela

HHB: How long have you been in the business?

HHB: About twenty years.

HHB: Isn't it true they call you "Mr. Greeting Card?"

HHB: Aw, shucks. You can call me Mr. Card.

HHB: Isn't it also true that you've had over three thousand cards published?

HHB: Aw shucks. (I love self-interviews.)

HHB: What initially attracted you to the greeting card business?

HHB: Initially the low pay and long hours. But I think I stuck with it for the fame.

HHB: Do you think greeting cards are important?

HHB: I put them right up there with plastic pocket protectors and gold bowling balls. Seriously though, I think they're probably more important than they ever were. With the appearance of the Alternative greeting card, I think they're becoming a legitimate art form. Whatever that means.

HHB: What is the Alternative greeting card?

HHB: Originally the term referred to any greeting card not produced by the big four or five greeting card companies, but it now means almost any generic, nontraditional greeting card. The Alternative greeting card is a product of the anti-establishment sentiment of the sixties. It was this sentiment that provided the market for the small entrepreneurial greeting card companies of the late sixties and early seventies. However, the Alternative card itself is anything from super-slick photography to extremely crude artwork.

HHB: What kind of illustration do you do?

HHB: Almost entirely Humorous.

HHB: What tips do you have for anyone trying to sell artwork?

HHB: In big letters, TRY FOR A ROYALTY ARRANGEMENT! Don't underestimate the value of your work. Why not share in its success? In addition I would go for an upfront payment or advance against royalties.

HHB: Any other tips?

HHB: Study the market. Go to card shops. Buy some of the cards that you admire. Incorporate those elements of design you admire in your work. Don't copy, but use what's successful as a teacher. Keep going back to the card shops.

HHB: How do you do your artwork? What size? What materials do you use, etc.?

HHB: I use 2-ply vellum surface bristol board for both black line and color. Let me explain. First, I draw the design in ink. From this I have an acetate positive shot (this is a clear sheet of plastic with the design in black). I then do my color directly over this on another sheet of bristol over a lightbox. You could do both ink and color on the same sheet of bristol, but the black line won't be as solid when it's printed.

HHB: What kind of pen do you use?

HHB: I use technical pens, with point sizes .25mm and .35mm

HHB: Paint?

HHB: Mostly gouache. But I also use watercolors and watercolor dyes. I use both a brush and an airbrush.

HHB: What are the most important things to consider when doing Humorous illustration?

HHB: The proper expression for the sentiment and eye contact with the recipient, when appropriate. They both sound extremely obvious, but I'm always surprised how often artists don't do either. In the latter case, whether it's an animal, a carrot, or an alien being, if there's no eye contact, the card will not sell no matter how funny the copy. It's like a television announcer reading cue cards instead of looking directly into the camera.

HHB: Well, is this it?

HHB: Pretty much.

HHB: Twenty years and this is it?

HHB: Yeah. Good luck to all you punters. I've got to go now. This is my bowling night and I'm dying to try out my new gold bowling ball. Old habits die hard.

Created by Harry H. Brown © Harry H. Brown

HO! HO! HO!

MERRY CHRISTMAS

This example of a Humorous Christmas design by Harry Brown illustrates the Sight Gag. Santa is a strong and traditional subject for Christmas cards.

UNDERSTATEMENT

Humor almost tickles through the use of Understatement. The recipient knows the sender means to say much, much more and the restraint sets up a kind of tension that enhances the humor. The illustration of the fortieth Birthday card, shown here, is a wonderful example of this device.

EXAGGERATION

Exaggeration creates a sense of absurdity about any situation, as is adeptly illustrated in the example shown below left. This approach can be taken even further into the unreal realm of the non sequitur as in the illustration shown opposite, bottom. It's difficult to judge this sort of humor because of the high degree of subjectivity involved. Go cautiously here, as it's easy to talk yourself into believing that something you've done is funny when it may only be so to you. This especially is an area where you should ask others for opinions about your work as suggested earlier in this chapter. Remember to listen carefully and objectively. An often repeated opinion probably has merit. Don't get mad at your critics. *You need them! Try* to be objective, remain flexible, and keep trying.

This is an example of using Understatement to create a Humorous card. Even the design itself is restrained in the attitude of the character, giving nothing away, and, therefore, adding to the tension of a very funny fortieth Birthday card.

And I'm not !

Whenever possible, try to capitalize on the current popularity of a trend. This example of Exaggeration in creating a Blank Humorous Card plays on the vogue that sushi enjoys in this country. The Exaggeration in this example goes beyond the basic idea of the card into the rendering where the size of the fish and the type of people shown are also exaggerated. Even the pose of the people in the water resembles bobbers, adding to the hilarity.

This example of Exaggeration to create a Humorous card also incorporates the Sight Gag. The complete absurdity of both design and editorial, beginning with a television ad and applying it in such a nonsensical way to a "Birthday from Both of Us" card is very effective.

and you're not.
Happy Birthday from both of us.

The design carries the joke for the Sight Gag for the most part. You might consider putting it to use on a Christmas card. The illustration of the wind-up mice, shown here, is an excellent example of a Sight Gag on the cover complemented by an editorial on the inside of the card.

Created by Eva Szela   Kit & Kaboodle™ © Eva Szela

IT'S NICE TO HAVE SOME FRIENDS

VISIT YOU WHEN YOU'RE NOT

FEELING WELL.

HOPE YOU'RE FEELING BETTER.

Creating Humorous cards is fun. There's a delightful note of absurdity in this example of a Sight Gag of wind-up mice as get well visitors. Note the innate benevolent niceness in the styling of the cat. The near Whimsical styling makes this look particularly appealing to women.

PLAY ON WORDS

Puns are the most common use of the Play-on-Words device. One example is a woman with a chicken on her head illustrated on the cover of a card, with the words, "Not tonight, dear" and inside "I'm in a fowl mood." The possibilities for puns are endless (if not painless). Be sure to look around and study what's already been done so you're not accidentally tripping over someone else's work. Also be aware that puns, in general, were very heavily done in the seventies and early eighties and have been done less since. Their popularity may increase again, but in the interim be aware you risk seeming dated with this approach.

The Play on Words can be illustrated with a very light touch. You can certainly come up with several applications of this sort of wit.

**Happy Birthday
to a classic!**

This is another example of the spot design layout solution as it's applied to a Humorous greeting card. Here the word play device is combined with the design to create a light and complimentary Birthday card. Note the interesting and refreshing use of color. The size of the design in relation to the size of the card adds to its dynamism.

SURPRISE

The Surprise may be one of the most popular devices used to create Humorous greeting cards. You lead the reader in one direction, as on the cover of the illustration shown on page 104 and then bonk them with the Surprise when the card is opened! The illustration shown here is an exciting combination of both the Surprise *and* the Slam against a group examined earlier. Surprise can also be combined with Understatement. The illustration shown opposite is an excellent example of Surprise used specifically in a woman-to-woman card. You can also capitalize on style to create the Surprise.

Surprise can be put to use on a risqué card as in the example shown far right. Risqué cards are very popular. This group should not be confused with more x-rated versions. Risqué is an approach that hints rather than specifies. If the area, as a whole, appeals to you, you should give it some thought because it's very popular.

Created by Eva Szela BLAB!™ © Eva Szela

This example of a Humorous greeting card illustrates the use of both Surprise and the Slam against a group. Note the Sophisticated styling in this very woman-to-woman Friendship card.

GIVE HIM A ONE WAY TICKET

TO GUAM.

This example of Surprise in a Humorous card strikes a chord of sympathy and support in this wonderful woman-to-woman Birthday card. Note the chatty posture of the character on the cover and the cup on the table, both subtle suggestions of close friendship and long conversations.

This illustration is an excellent example of Surprise used so that the viewer is led to believe a tremendous compliment is about to be paid. Instead the idea is turned around into a risqué compliment rather than a general one and the rhythm of writing is changed as well. Study the manner in which the editorial goes from the lofty and the abstract on the cover to the low-down and specific on the inside. This technique augments the impact of the Surprise.

Another birthday and you're still not married. What are you waiting for — someone who's good-looking, rich, sensitive, witty and perfect ??

H. Lehrer

I like you because of your lofty ideals, your sense of fairness, and your keen analytical wit.

... Me too.

HAVE A HAPPY BIRTHDAY!

THE FACT THAT YOU'RE

A GREAT LAY HAS LITTLE

OR NOTHING TO DO

WITH IT!

❝ I have been in the greeting card business for about fifteen years. A few months ago I left as the Art Director for Recycled Paper Products, Inc. to begin free-lancing. The business found me. I was a printmaker working in woodcut and intaglio processes with no thought of commercial design. At that time the greeting card industry produced little that seemed compatible with what I was doing. When Recycled Paper Products expressed an interest in my work, I was pleased to have the sales. Happily, people liked my work. The association grew into a full time, creatively rewarding career.

The Alternative card is something new. It's important because it brings change, expands the possibilities for the field, and affords the buying public the opportunity to be personally expressive with their selections. When looking for a design for Recycled's lines we looked for a creative thinker willing to work hard, needing little guidance, and capable of continuing to be innovative in a long-term working relationship. The art must be fresh and original, yet have some degree of polish and sophistication. Individual style, the ability to write, and a never-ending imagination are equally important. A sense of humor is vital for all Recycled's creative people, no matter what their style. The product is light hearted. The goal is to help people keep in contact with friends. Sharing a laugh at life's foibles with a friend seems like an excellent way to communicate.

The most important things for a greeting card illustrator to keep in mind are:

- A card is a product that is used for communication between two people.

- Its look must be different in some way from all other cards already on the market.

- Be objective. Would you send the card you are designing? Do the concept and the illustration represent something that is preferable to the thousand or so others on the racks?

All areas of greeting cards are fair game today. People buy and send cards to address the most intimate, most painful, or upsetting situations in relationships. Cards seem to have moved from an aid to communication to *the* communication. The explosion of acceptable card sending situations illustrates how healthy, vital, and growing the industry is.

Greeting cards definitely offer special opportunities for artists' creativity. There are no limitations, really. Recycled looks for distinctive images. The search is for styles that are individual. The only constraint is that the artist must remember the use of the product he or she is illustrating. Beyond that, it's open for individual creativity. The Alternative card has opened an important source of illustration opportunity. In the case of Recycled Paper Products, the artist is expected to start with his/her own concepts and carry them to finished art. Little editing is done and the preference is to work with people who don't need or want it. Artistic self-expression is a necessity, not a luxury with us.

Greeting card illustration is a highly competitive field. It takes at least 18 months to see the rewards for hard work. But few commercial areas offer the freedom that one enjoys with cards. It is a field where individuality is encouraged and nurtured.

Greeting cards are important. Every form of communication is important. A card that does it with flair, variety, and fun is even more important. That one person takes the time to send a card to another person is an example of human caring. Let's call greeting cards a readily available source of emotional nourishment. ❞

Close your eyes, and pucker your lips.

It's time to kiss another year good-bye.

Happy Birthday

The element of Surprise is fun to work with in creating Humorous greeting cards. In this example published by Recycled Paper Products the editorial works in close conjunction with the design to lead the viewer to believe that this is a Romantic or risqué card. Of course, the Surprise is the age Slam.

SHARED JOKE

The Shared Joke is not strictly a Humorous device. Rather it's a means of presentation that has recently come into vogue in Humorous cards and is enjoying tremendous popularity. The entire joke is contained on the cover of the card, no sending situation is specified, and sending the card is prompted chiefly by a desire to share the joke. The illustration of the nerds shown here is a good example of this kind of card. Go back and look over the illustration on page 99 for another highly successful version of this technique.

This illustration is another good example of the Slam against a group, used as a Shared Joke in creating a Humorous blank greeting card. There is no specific sending situation. The reason for sending the card is the desire to show a friend a joke you think is funny.

SEASONAL HUMOR

All the devices you've just examined (and, of course, any new ones you invent!) can be applied to Seasonal greeting cards. The humor may be softened for certain seasons or occasions. Mother's Day, for example, is a good opportunity for humor. Love or gratitude will usually be couched in the joke. An example can be seen in the illustration shown here. Father's Day is another good opportunity for holiday humor. However, the humor is again light hearted and loving, frequently focusing on traditional concepts of fatherhood. An example of a Father's Day card is shown opposite.

Christmas is the biggest holiday for greeting cards. There is certainly an opportunity for Humorous Christmas cards. Some popular themes are holiday stress, anything relating to Santa, reindeer, elves, chimneys, sleighs, mistletoe, shopping, gifts, merriness, and good wishes. Humorous Christmas cards are usually created from the secular perspective of the holiday. You risk offense by making light of the Religious aspects of this holiday.

Valentine's Day is *very* suited to Humorous greeting cards, especially Slams and Insults. The illustration of the woman, shown far right, is an interesting example of both the device of Surprise and that of the Slam in a Humorous Valentine. Themes are usually love-related or Valentine-related as in "Valentine, be mine . . . nobody else will have you."

Every holiday presents a Humorous opportunity. Let your common sense be your guide. If the holiday is based on a Religious event, tread lightly and carefully so as not to give offense. Otherwise, simply address whatever the basis for the holiday is, try out a few of the devices for creating humor that you've explored in this chapter, and have a go at the holiday of your choice. The jokes are there. Have fun with them! If you think you're funny, you probably are.

Mom, you will really appreciate this card...

H. Lehrer

...it's already clean, neatly folded, AND wrinkle-free!

This is an excellent example of a Humorous Mother's Day card. The humor is soft, the device is Surprise, and the subject matter is Mom and flowers, very Feminine in appeal.

106

This is an excellent example of a Humorous Father's Day card. Traditional Dad roles are the topic and Surprise is used for effective impact in this highly successful card.

This example of a Humorous Valentine shows a wonderful use of both Surprise and the Slam. The Slam and the Insult are both very effective and popular devices for this particular holiday.

...or financial assistance.

"... WOULD IT SPOIL THIS MOMENT

FOR YOU IF I THREW UP?"

6

PLANNING YOUR
COLORS
FOR IMPACT

COLOR is important. Always consider it carefully. It's a good idea to establish your palette at the same time as you plan your subject matter, begin your layout, either write or consider your editorial, and determine your medium. Color can have significant impact on the success of your greeting card.

Certain kinds of color can limit the uses to which your design may be put. For example, as we determined in Chapter 2, browns and deep, dark colors have a Masculine connotation. This does not mean that these colors may only be used on Masculine cards; it does mean that Masculine cards done without this kind of color palette may not be readily accepted. Conversely, soft pastels are equated with Feminine designs. While it may be true that certain colors within the softer range may also be right for Sophisticated stylings, it's also true that if you want a decidedly Feminine styling like Sweetly Charming to work well, you should almost certainly use soft pastel colors.

Brights are another matter entirely. These kinds of color are very broad in their appeal. They can be Feminine; they are cheery and will work with

any sending situation (except Sympathy): Birthday, certainly, Friendship, yes. The illustration shown here is a truly beautiful example of how color can be used effectively. The step-by-step demonstration at the end of this chapter illustrates how bright colors can be used to create a Sophisticated Friendship card with liquid watercolors.

Greeting card color is different from other color. Some of the larger corporations have gone so far as to formulate special inks in the pink and aqua ranges to help reproduce this very warm, almost sweet, color so characteristic of greeting cards. Pink is extremely important.

Within the area of Juveniles, primary and secondary colors are the rule. (Not to be confused with brights, these are red, blue, and yellow in their most basic tones, with a few secondary green, purple, and orange accents). When it comes to Baby, there is dissension among the ranks. Traditionally soft, soft pastels were the rule (pink for girls, blue for boys, yellow for neither or both). Now primary colors are favored in some quarters as being more stimulating for Baby. A lot of nursery products are now offered in primaries. This trend creates a dilemma in Baby Congratulation cards. For example, the person buying the card may not have children (or young ones) and thus may not be privy to this new color scheme. To this person, primaries in Baby may seem weird. For the most part, traditional pastels seem to be holding their own.

Keep the sending situation in mind when choosing color. Sometimes specific colors are *required* for certain situations. For example, a Silver Wedding Anniversary card must be silver at least in feeling, if not actually a metallic silver material. The same holds true for Golden Wedding Anniversary. Christmas *almost always* must be red and green. If one or the other or both of these colors do not predominate, they should at least be represented somewhere in the design. Bright blue also enjoys some popularity at Christmas, but falls way behind the other two.

Holidays that occur during specific seasons often adopt colors present in nature at the time of their celebration. Easter colors are usually purple, yellow, and green as are the daffodils, lilacs, and crocuses blooming at that time of year. Halloween and Thanksgiving colors are those of fall leaves: orange for Halloween and rusts, oranges, and browns for Thanksgiving.

Research color just as you would subject matter, trends, or other ideas. (More on Research can be found in Chapter 9.) It is a fascinating area and has just as much importance as every other facet of greeting card creation. Have fun with it. Play around with it. Try intellectualizing color, but also give your instincts a chance, just go with your gut feelings, and see what happens. Set up a color file and keep pieces of color that you like ready for your next design.

Color is subjective. Look at the illustration shown on page 108 as an example of a color palette that in the old days of greeting card design would have been rejected: the extensive use of black in a Whimsical styling. Black was perceived as a downer. Yet here you can see what a rich and totally charming look can be achieved when some of the rules are broken. Color can be the cornerstone for a whole new look that's just you!

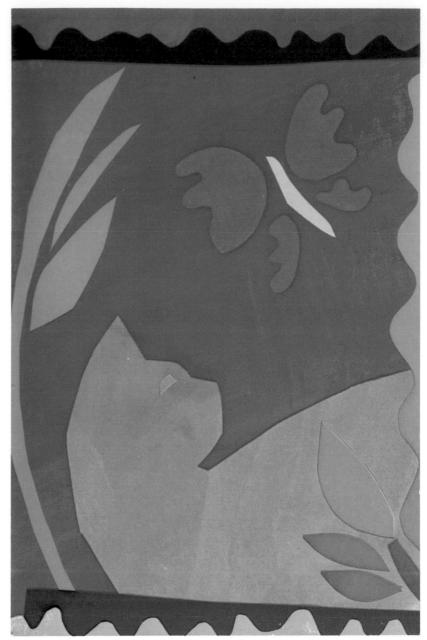

May your special day
be filled with beauty...
may your heart be filled
with happiness.

Happy Birthday

This bright color palette is both adventurous and beautiful. Note the unique combination of greens and the unusual, almost tropical feeling of the color in general, totally appropriate to this Sophisticated styling of a cat and butterfly.

For all the little things you do. . .
Thanks!

This is an example of the kind of bright pastels which work very well on greeting cards. Here the color is used to Feminize a Humorous card.

This beautiful use of bright color works so well for a very general and cheery Birthday card.

*W*ishing you
in the warmest way
A fun-filled,
sun-filled happy day!

DEMONSTRATION NINE

USING LIQUID

WATERCOLORS TO

CREATE A BRIGHTLY

COLORED

FRIENDSHIP CARD

Brilliant colors and transparency are the main characteristics of liquid watercolors (or dyes). They produce a delicate, tissue-thin feel, an advantage when creating designs for Feminine appeal. In this example of using liquid watercolors, your sending situation is Friendship, Missing You. Only a person can warmly and endearingly illustrate the feeling of this card and its message. The cover will say, "without you . . ." and the inside "even sunshine's no fun." Because of its extreme primitiveness, the styling is Sophisticated.

1

2

3

1. *Determine your card size and begin to sketch your design. The character is primitive in styling. Note how simplistically both she and her surroundings are done.*

2. *Transfer your rough sketch to the paper upon which you'll be doing your finish. Stay flexible. Note that the sun has been moved to the left side to better balance the design. Keep in mind that watercolors are highly transparent. It isn't always possible to erase pencil line through them as it is with gouache. Lighten the lines now by pressing your kneaded eraser over the line and picking it up.*
Plan your color. Use colors close to the primaries in keeping with the bright simplicity of the look. In addition to the bright colors you'll need to develop a flesh tone for the hands, face, and legs and a soft gray for outlining. Begin to paint in your colors.

3. *Get all the color down in simple, single, basic strokes using one coat of paint only. Take care to paint inside the remaining lines and then go back in and erase out all the linework around each color after you've painted it in. Lay masking tape in any areas where you think color will bleed outside the picture area in order to control your paint. This design will have a white background and only the sun and grasses are likely to extend beyond the picture area, so mask out those areas with tape.*

4. *Come back in with the same colors, adding a single second layer of paint in some areas to create shading as in her face and dress and in the flower centers. Note how transparent these colors are and how much the second layer of paint adds to the effect. Paint her hair yellow and outline everything in either gray or a darker color that's compatible with the area around it (orange and gray for the sun and her hat). Add polka dots to her tie and paint the lettering gray. Erase all the remaining lines, remove the masking tape, and you're finished!*

without you...

7

USING
BASIC DESIGN
TECHNIQUES

L<small>IKE NOW</small>.

I <small>LOVE YOU</small>.

This combination of asymmetric pattern and border is an effective attention-getting device. Remember, it's the design that makes them pick it up, and the editorial that makes them put it back. This design will stand out in the rack as well as appeal to the young, active woman of today.

THERE is a difference between drawing the subject matter for a greeting card and designing the drawing *and* the entire space around it. These two are entirely different functions. To do an isolated drawing floating in space meets one challenge. If the drawing's a good one, terrific! But that's not the whole job of creating a greeting card. This chapter examines the design of the card—the different ways of breaking up the space on the card. The general ones will be discussed.

FULL BLEED

Although the term may sound awful, a full bleed means that the image, images, or colors are composed so that they fill the entire space. The illustrations opposite and on the bottom of page 16, are full-bleed designs. The Appendix: Media and Tools provides an explanation of the term itself and its technical implications.

The asymmetrical placement of the lilies creates tension in contrast with the symmetry of the border, which in reproduction was formal gold foil. The use of a blue background lends an air of formality, a note entirely correct for this Blank Card's very general, and therefore highly useful, direction.

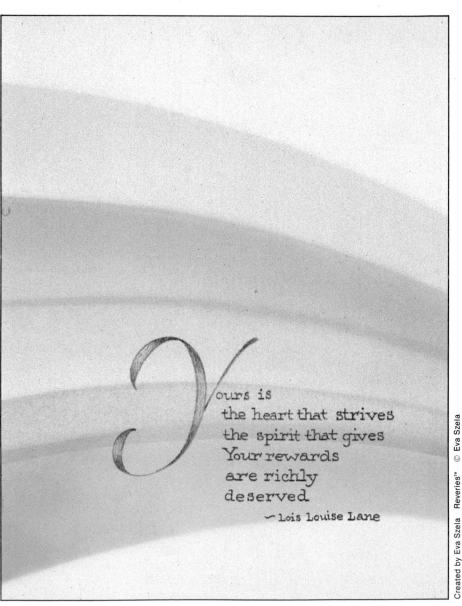

Yours is
the heart that strives
the spirit that gives
Your rewards
are richly
deserved
~ Lois Louise Lane

In this example of a full-bleed design the soft sweep of the diagonal and the unique nature of the rainbow, in combination with the congratulatory nature of the editorial, all go together to make this Blank Inspirational Card a successful one.

BORDERS

The border is an interesting layout solution for a more contained or controlled feeling. The illustration shown opposite top is a lovely formal use of a border in conjunction with an unusually balanced Realistic Floral design. You can also create a border and then break it for interest with an element from the center design area. The baby illustration shown right uses the absence of design in the outer area of the card to create a white border and then pulls one tiny element from the center area and places it in the lower right-hand corner of this border for interest.

WISHING YOU BRIGHT AND HAPPY

MOMENTS WITH YOUR NEW LITTLE

BUNDLE OF SUNSHINE

This is another example of using a border design. The soft yellow background for a Baby Congratulations card makes it work for babies of either gender. Note that a tiny element from the center of the design is echoed in the lower right-hand corner of the border.

Spot designs are common especially in certain kinds of Humorous cards. A spot design is one which is vignetted or floating in the space around it. The resulting simplicity has an appeal all its own and this approach has met with terrific success. While this type of design may appear to be easy, a lot of development can be needed in the simplest styling. The illustration shown below is an example of an exquisite Whimsical styling using the spot design technique to create delicate accents on both the cover and the inside.

Patterns are fun and offer exciting ways to experiment with design elements on greeting cards. You could use colorful, energetic hearts in a loose pattern, far right, or introduce a Pattern into a border to create a contemporary Memphis-influenced Whimsical styling, page 114. An example of a pattern in a border is in the illustration shown right. Another type of pattern is shown in the following step-by-step demonstration.

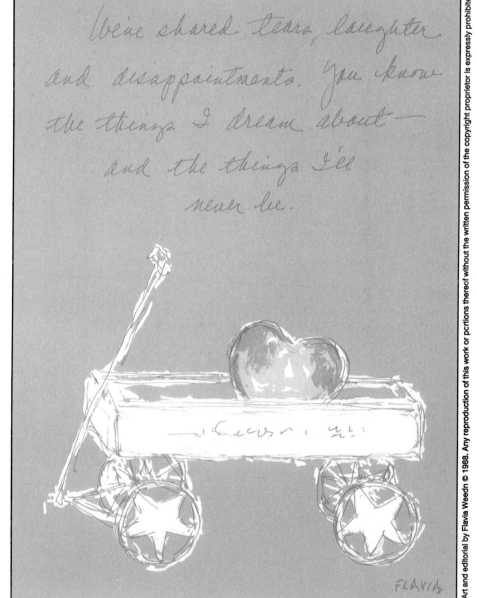

The spot design is a wonderfully simple layout device. In this example the entire card is involved simply by using a background color. The elegant Whimsical styling works beautifully with the intimate and conversational editorial.

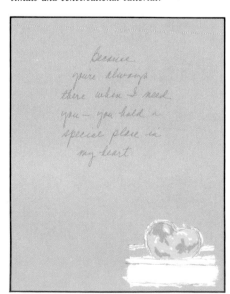

The use of both pattern and border here is consistent with the Graphic styling of the Baby Congratulations card. The design is sweet and delicate even though its manner is flat and hardedged.

Patterns provide some terrific layout possibilities. In this example of a use of one, the bright color and Stylized look in combination with the very general editorial make it just right for innumerable Friendship sending situations. The pattern extends all the way around the back of the card for a little something extra.

On your new arrival!

DEMONSTRATION TEN

STYLING A

SOPHISTICATED

PATTERN WITH

FELT TIP

MARKERS

What fun to create a very Stylized and Sophisticated pattern of birthday candles and flowers with soft-tipped markers! You have a multitude of different kinds of felt markers to choose from today. All kinds of points are available (more coming all the time) and the colors are bright or deep or pastel. There are even waterbased colors! In this example you will explore markers with flexible brushlike tips. Your sending situation is general Feminine Birthday. There is no copy on the cover and the inside says, "Happy Birthday!" This design is inspired by both subject and medium.

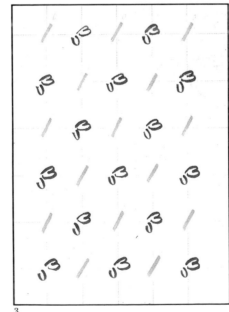

1

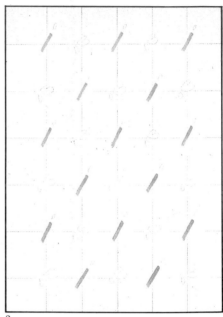

2

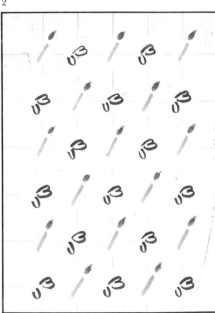

3

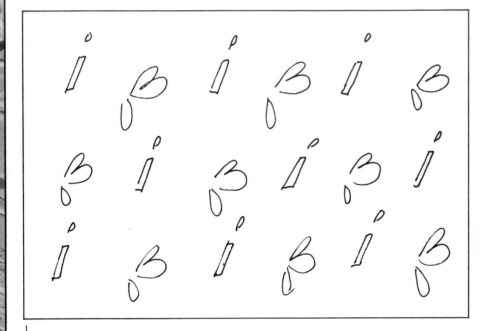

4

1. *As a thought occurs to you, jot it down. Always carry a little notepad or sketchbook. Get in the habit of doing this (if you don't already) because inspirations do go away! Note the pattern sketch here. Bright pastels will emphasize the femininity and fun of this card. Lots of white space around these colors will keep the feeling clean and perky. Every medium has limitations. With markers you're strictly limited to the colors available. Since the colors are transparent, some overlay is possible. But since the second color will pick up some of the first the practice is not advised. Therefore, it's good to plan for the limitations.*

2. *Measure the approximate space between elements in your original sketch. The horizontal spaces are about ¾" apart and the vertical about 1". Determine the size of your card. Mark it on the paper on which you intend to do your finish. Then measure out the vertical and horizontal spaces. Since the ¾" spaces do not fall evenly on the width of the card, leave a 1" margin on either side to give your pattern room to breathe. Now go into the grid you've created*

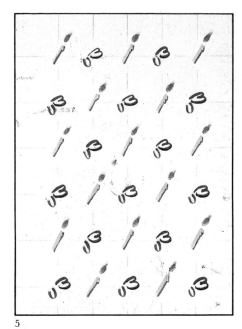

5

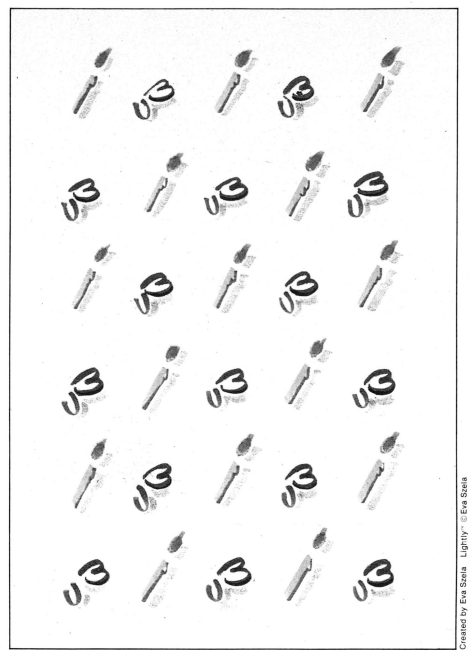

6

*and very lightly sketch in the candles and flowers.
Because the design is on a slant remember to
keep the elements at a similar angle. Take your
kneaded eraser and go over each design element,
pressing the eraser and lifting it to lighten the
linework so it's just visible enough to follow.
Keeping the angle of the marker the same throughout, go into the design with a simple, single stroke
and color each candle light blue. Erase the lines
from each color as you go.*

3. *Next do the flower. Take a few practice runs
on scrap paper to establish the angle at which to
hold the marker tip. Again keep the angle consistent throughout and color the flower shapes in
light pink. Now do the leaves in dark green.
There is no right or wrong angle with which to
hold your pen. Just find one you like and stick
to it as you do each element in the pattern.*

4. *Using a fine-line yellow marker, outline the
candle flames in simple strokes. If you want a
very naive look, stop right here, erase out your
pencil work, and you're finished. However, a
few additional strokes will make the look more
eighties — Soft Tech, Memphis, or New
Wave — depending on your perspective. Color in
each candle flame with the yellow brush-like
marker. Extend the stroke a little beyond the top
of each yellow outline already drawn. Now
you've begun to add an element of depth to the
design.*

5. *Add darker blue along the under edge of each
candle, creating a tiny drip effect at the top end
of each candle for fun realism. Now add the
darker pink to the undersides of the flowers.*

6. *Take the neutral beige, and add a drop
shadow to each element in the design. Notice
that this shadow does not touch the existing
elements but is a little distance from each one.
The shadow can be either in front of or behind
each element. Erase all remaining pencil
linework. Your sophisticated Feminine Birthday
pattern is now completed!*

Created by Eva Szela   Lightly™ © Eva Szela

The use of type, calligraphy, or lettering as the focal point of the design with no person, animal, or object depicted is very general in appeal. Each card works for many different kinds of people depending on what the editorial says. The illustration shown on page 123 is an example of just such a card. This is a Religious Birthday that could be sent to a man or a woman, a younger or an older person, which makes it a highly sendable greeting card. You might want to create a Sophisticated Mother's Day design with lettering as the focal point. The illustration shown here, with its bright Birthday color and bold type solution on the cover balanced by a full-color, full-bleed deisgn on the inside of the card, is another unique layout using the editorial predominant solution. See Chapter 8 for more on lettering.

Many approaches to greeting card design will work. These are just a few examples of some of the more popular ones in use today. If you think your card may be produced commercially, it is a good idea to design it so that the lettering appears in the top third of the front of the card. Some cards are displayed on racks where one shelf overlaps the one behind it. In this case, the top third is all that's seen by the consumer at point of purchase.

Whatever layout option you choose, play around with several solutions. Stay loose and try a variety of combinations until you find the one that best suits the card you're putting together.

happy birthday

In this example of the editorial predominant layout, type has been used in an inventive manner. Bright colors are just right for a very general Birthday card. The real fun is the element of interest on the inside of the card, in the absence of an inside editorial, a unique twist.

This example of using the editorial as the focal point of a design is particularly interesting because of the unusual means by which the color is introduced. Trying for special effects can be one of the many fun challenges of working with calligraphy and lettering.

"Thou crownest the year with thy goodness. . . ."
Psalm 65:11

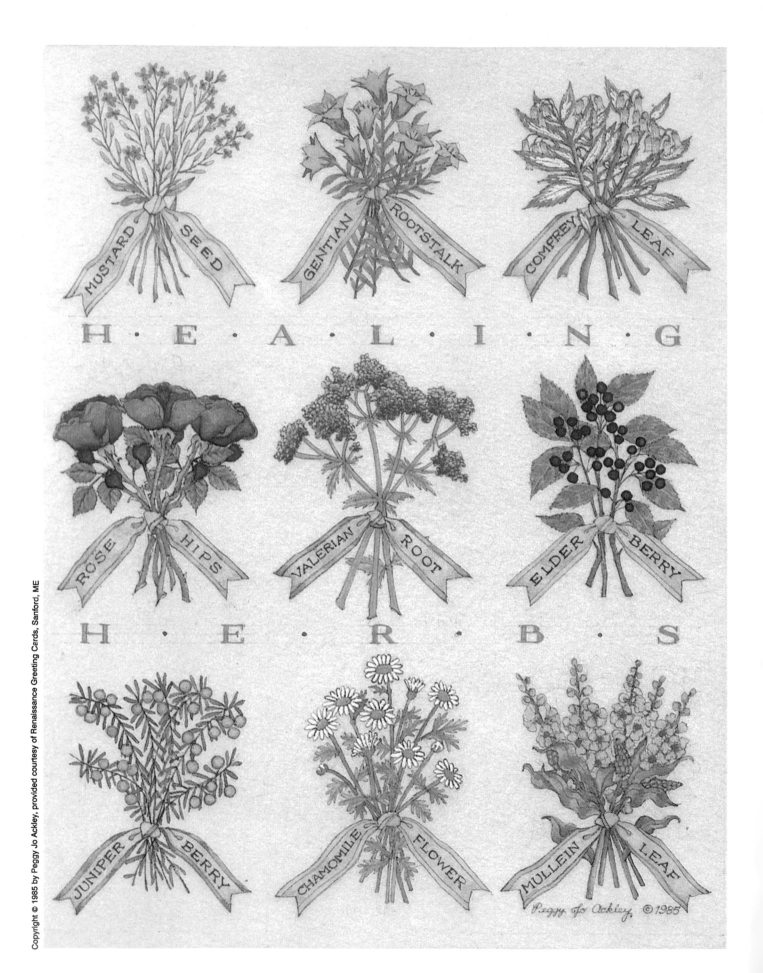

8
DESIGNING WITH WORDS

Sending you healing thoughts,
in hopes that you'll soon be well.

This illustration is a classic in its very general styling and appeal, so the serif lettering form is used appropriately here. The lettering sets off the design and identifies the sending situation.

IF YOUR greeting has an editorial and you're interested in lettering it yourself, then this chapter is of importance to you. Lettering is as integral to the design as is color, subject, and composition. Lettering *is* the design to the same degree that *any other* visual element is within it. They must work together, and well, if your design is going to be successful. Consider again all the different styles of greeting card art you explored in Chapter 2. There may not be as many different styles of lettering, but certain kinds of lettering are more appropriate to certain designs than others. This does not mean there are hard and fast rules about which lettering goes with which styles, but it does mean that you should study the various ways lettering is done and develop a feel for what works and what doesn't and why.

SERIF

Serif letters include all Roman style letters that have small score lines at the beginnings and ends of all the main strokes. This small line is called a "serif." The lettering in the illustration shown opposite is an excellent example of serif letterforms. This is a classic look. It's warmer in feeling than the sans serif group, but cooler than script. It's very easy to read. Many different kinds of serif lettering styles are used. Study all forms of printed matter (especially greeting cards) with this in mind and begin to see the tremendous variety of styles in use as well as the various ways each style can be used. Many serif typefaces are available for you to review at your local typesetter's or printer's.

SANS SERIF

Sans Serif letters include all Roman style letters that do not have serifs. The illustration with cats, shown right, in its printed form, below, is an excellent example of the sans serif lettering style. As a group, this style is perceived to be newer. It's cooler in feeling and very easy to read. There are a lot of different sans serif lettering styles. Study all forms of printed matter (especially greeting cards) with sans serif styling in mind and begin to see the many different ways this kind of lettering is used. As with serif styles, here too the weight, size, specific style, and manner of reproduction all combine to determine whether or not a particular sans serif styling might be right for your design. Meet with a typesetter or printer in your area to review styles. These people will be happy to offer suggestions.

Sans serif lettering is cooler in feeling than the serif style. Note in this charmingly Whimsical illustration how the sans serif lettering is warmed, because it is reproduced in pink. The effect is soft and just right in combination with leaping kitties.

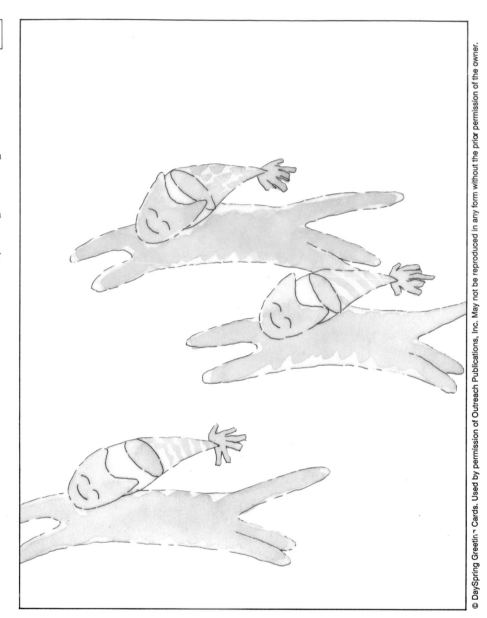

SCRIPT

Script includes all lettering styles designed to imitate handwriting. Sometimes they actually *are* handwriting. The style is characterized by the fact that all the letters within each word connect to one another. The illustration with the lily, shown right, contains a beautiful example of the use of script. This style of lettering is perhaps most closely associated with traditional greeting cards. It is very soft and Feminine in feeling. It is less easy to read than the other styles, but it's much, much warmer. Only you can judge when that is most appropriate to your design.

Within each of the above three groups a further distinction should be made: the difference between formal and casual versions. This distinction is more important today than ever before. A few years ago, *only* formal lettering could be found on any card except a Humorous one. Now casual lettering abounds and is even seen as an asset because of the warmth and personalness it can lend a card. The illustration of the Mother's Day card, shown on page 128, makes this point most effectively. Casual lettering also encourages more artists to develop the art of lettering. It isn't all that difficult to begin with your own printing, for example, and do it carefully over and over, trying always for the most readability possible while not forsaking style. The illustration of a bon voyage card, shown on page 128, is another good example of applied casual lettering.

Formal lettering, on the other hand, is a good deal dressier. It's also a little cooler in feeling. It establishes slightly more distance between the sender and the recipient. It is completely appropriate and desirable with certain kinds of designs. The illustration of the Birthday card, shown on page 129, is a good example of one of these. Hand-done formal lettering takes a good deal of practice and skill. If you don't want to or can't invest the time, there are other ways to get lettering for your design.

The graceful delicacy of this lily works in harmony with the sensitive script lettering to create a feeling of femininity that is entirely appropriate and desirable in this Friendship sending situation.

This example of casual lettering is an excellent example to study of how delicate and sensitive this kind of lettering can be when it's appropriate. Note the air of distinction this design achieves without giving up any of its warmth or Femininity.

This casual lettering style is based on a hand-printed Roman sans serif. It works perfectly with the casual and personal style of the artwork.

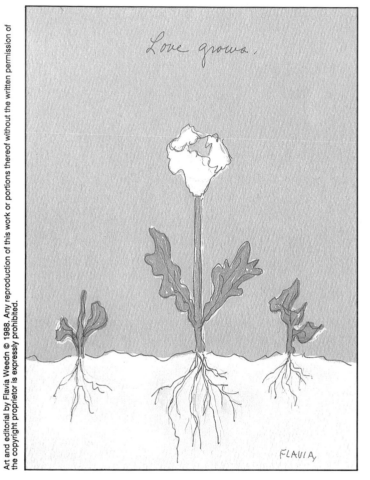

This is an example of a lovely use of formal lettering that is beautifully in balance with the Oriental design below it.

May you have
a wonderful birthday
filled with
every special blessing . . .
overflowing
with
every lovely thing!

"Now to Him who is able to do exceedingly abundantly
above all that we ask or think. . . ."
Ephesians 3:20 NKJV

Transfer type is printed on sheets of film. It is rubbed off, letter by letter, on to any surface you like. It's available at any artist supply store in a wide variety of styles and sizes. Its chief disadvantage is that it's vulnerable to scraping and chipping after it's been applied. Spraying with fixative after application can help alleviate this problem, but it's always best to handle your lettering with care.

TYPESETTING

Having lettering set for you can be a lot of fun. Shop around in your area for a printer or typesetter whose work you like. Sit down with these people and go over the styles available. They will help you with sizes, weights, and related issues if you give them an idea of what you're trying to achieve. This could mean simply showing them a sketch and indicating generally what kind of lettering you're interested in and where you'd like the lettering to go in your layout. Or if you want to try a design where the lettering is predominant, then you might pick a typeface you like. Order it and design around it. The following step-by-step demonstration shows a design that was put together in just this way.

In this example of designing with typesetting you will see a Christmas card evolve. First write your editorial or have someone write it for you if you prefer. For this design "The season is upon us!" will be on the cover and "May yours be full of warmth and joy" will be on the inside.

The season is upon us!

1.

1. *Select a typeface you like. Determine a size and weight and order it. An interesting example of a sans serif style of lettering is shown here. What you get back from the typesetter will look something like this. You should also get a solid black copy, which is the one you'll ultimately use.*

2. *Play around with some Christmas design ideas. Try a layout or however many suit you using the elements you've selected.*

3. *Select the layout you like most. Here a pattern on the front and back of the card is appealing, especially in combination with this lettering. Cut out your type and paste it in position. You can use rubber cement, which will allow you to move the type around later (with the help of rubber cement thinner). Or when you have the type set you can ask to have it waxed so all you have to do is lay it down and press and it will stay. It can also be moved around if you like. Since this design will be printed in the two Christmas colors, do one finished ink drawing for each color. This is the green finish. See the Appendix for more information about pens.*

4. *On another piece of paper, do the portion of your design you want printed in red. Include crop marks in the corners of both drawings to indicate the edges of your card.*

2.

3.

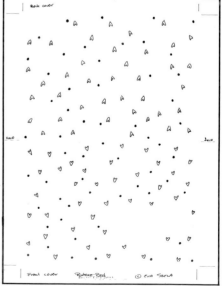

4.

The season is upon us!

© Eva Szela

5

May yours be full of warmth and joy.

© Eva Szela

6

5. *Take these finishes to your printer. Work with the printer to make final choices about exactly which red and which green to print your design in. In just a few days you'll have a Christmas card! Here you can see the front and back of the printed card.*

6. *The design and lettering on the inside are kept simple.*

Through this demonstration you'll learn how to use your own hand-writing to create lettering for a card. Readability and retention of the desired character or style are your primary objectives.

1. *Determine your editorial. For this example you'll work with "Thank you." As spontaneously, as dashingly, as flashily as you can, write your editorial several times. Don't worry about readability at this point; just go for style and verve.*

2. *Draw a line with a straight edge (see the Appendix information about art supplies) on tracing paper. This will be a general guide only. Casual lettering should bounce around a little, so don't try to place each letter perfectly along this line. Pick your favorite letters from Step 1 and trace them carefully. Because eventually you will be drawing in these lines to look heavier, exaggerate and widen all the curves as you trace them. Also alter any letterforms to make them more readable. Retain the feeling of spontaneity and dash as you carefully trace the lettering.*

3. *Retrace the lettering. Only first draw a line on either side of the original line you traced. Study your original loose sketches to help you determine where each stroke should be thinner or thicker. Follow the subtle weight variations you made naturally in your first sketches. Exaggerate them when you thicken each stroke in this new tracing. Study what you've done for readability. Make changes to be certain what you've lettered so far reads easily and quickly.*

4. *Turn your tracing paper over on its backside where you can see the tracing in reverse. Trace the lines on the back of the tracing paper.*

5. *Turn the tracing paper over so that the lettering reads correctly. As you draw over your original lines, the lines on the back of the paper will transfer to the surface upon which you will do your finish. Lay the tracing paper face up on this paper and tape it down lightly with masking tape.*

Now go over the existing linework with a pencil, applying a little pressure as you go. One example of how lettering at this stage is applied to a greeting card can be seen in the demonstration on the airbrush on pages 24–25.

6. *Using a mechanical pen, ink in the linework. You now have a piece of finished lettering that you can have enlarged or reduced and that can be combined with artwork in much the same way as in the preceding demonstration of set type.*

© Eva Szela

HAND LETTERING

Hand lettering is very challenging and exciting to do. There are various degrees of difficulty in hand lettering. The easiest thing to do when first trying it out is to start with your own handwriting. Do it carefully so that it is very readable while still retaining the character or style you want. Build a "caption" (as the final printed editorial on the cover of greeting cards is sometimes called) around it. The step-by-step demonstration, left, illustrates how to work in just this manner.

Another lettering alternative is to hire someone to do it for you. If you are interested in this solution, ask around; your typesetter or printer may be able to point you in the right direction. Also try calligraphers and advertising agencies as well as schools, if there are any in your area with appropriate courses and students looking for work.

If you're an illustrator interested in having your work published commercially, don't misunderstand this chapter. It's not necessary for you to do your own lettering. Many greeting card companies, as a matter of course, expect to do that part of the job. Some don't, but not many. So if doing your own lettering doesn't appeal to you, all is not lost.

Lettering your own designs is a fun opportunity to retain complete control over the total look of your work. Try it before deciding it's not for you. You may find some surprises. It may turn out to be quite a stimulus to your creativity in its own right! Your own lettering can add to the uniqueness of any look you decide to develop.

9
RESEARCHING CARD TRENDS, INFLUENCES AND IDEAS

THROUGH research you can determine the trends and influences that affect greeting cards, in addition to developing ideas. Without research, you're nowhere. You may already have certain research habits. If not, begin now to clip and collect anything that catches your eye as well as whatever you determine to be pertinent after examining this chapter.

Establish a system for keeping your research that will make it easy to retrieve the information you've stored. This can mean filing by subject matter, color, market segment; the possibilities go on and on. Only you can determine which way works best for you. Try one system and be sure to reassess it after a few months or a year. If you find you're not using your research, determine why. Is it filed in a confusing way? Are you not gathering material that is right for you? Change your system accordingly: either *what* you're collecting, *how* you're collecting it, or how you're

storing it. Research is a valuable tool; you should be using it. If you're not, you're forcing yourself to do things the hard way.

There are different kinds of research. Which kind is right for you will depend on what kind of work you're doing. If you're into general florals, for example, your needs will be entirely different from someone who's interested in doing Humorous greeting cards. You can research art styles, techniques, trends, fads, subject matter, competition, color, editorials, lettering, market segments, and whatever else you feel you need to know or have access to when you begin to conceptualize, sketch, or plan your work. Examine the following suggestions; pull out what you think applies to you. Adapt these things to your own special needs. Remember that there is nothing right or wrong about the way in which you do research; there is only what works for you and what doesn't.

This lovely watercolor illustration was the result of a series of stages beginning with the designer taking his own reference photos through to the final color sketch. To see how this illustration evolved turn to page 139.

135

HOME FURNISHINGS AND WEARING APPAREL

Home furnishings and wearing apparel are of interest to women and women are the big consumers of greeting cards. While greeting cards are not fashionable in and of themselves, consider that the woman who will like or not like your design is influenced by everything around her everyday. If she is seeing certain style tendencies or colors and she feels that what she's seeing is correct or acceptable, it's logical to assume that she will feel comfortable with that style statement or color palette wherever she finds it. Being aware of what is currently acceptable to the average user of greeting cards can help you make smart choices when the time comes. One word of warning: When exploring this area, develop your awareness of the difference between fads and trends. Both seem to get a lot of bad press when it comes to certain kinds of product planning. There is often the fear that each has a lack of staying power. However, a fad is only a temporary success where splurges of direction, like fluorescent color, for example, come and go quickly (sometimes in as little as a year's time). A trend, in contrast, is a general direction in the marketplace. It behooves you to anticipate trends by paying attention to market phenomenon. Who's doing what in sheets and towels this year? Women's wear? And next year and the next? If you keep this up, you will develop a sense of what's coming and you can work toward the coming trends.

About eight years ago there was an acknowledged teddy bear trend in the marketplace. A year later there was a lot of talk about how the teddy bear trend had peaked and was over. At about the same time there was similar talk about Country. Both of these trends are still far from over. With quiet strength they continue to succeed. It's easy to understand because both represent deep emotional attachments to home, hearth, and warmth; these are concepts everyone wants to hold on to whether they exist in each individual's life or not.

WOMEN'S MAGAZINES

Women's magazines can be invaluable ways to let you know what's going on in other women's lives, minds, careers, and families. They contain trends in more than design, color, and style. They also provide philosophical trends to monitor. Keeping your ear to the ground in these areas will help you better understand women. Even if you are a woman, you should do research to get outside yourself and your immediate circle in order to remain flexible and open to new ideas. Look at magazines that you wouldn't ordinarily read. If you're traditional, look at upscale, slick publications. If you're upscale and slick, look at homey, craft-oriented, homemaking-oriented publications. *Remember the library!* It's an excellent source of all kinds of research materials.

ADVERTISEMENTS

Advertisements are all around you. Take advantage of them! Pay attention to the styles of artwork used to achieve fun, new effects. Study typefaces and lettering styles! Here is where you'll see exciting work done in all areas of design and writing. Advertising *is* the pulsebeat of America. Learn from it. Some of the major firms are spending fortunes developing ads to elicit a response from the same people who will respond to your greeting card. If the ad you're seeing can do that, what can you learn about *how* it's done that you can apply to your next card? This could be anything from a homey "Mom's-in-the-kitchen" idea to a fabulous Memphis pattern. And this is true of both print and television ads. Even radio ads can be an interesting resource for writing. Don't overlook old print ads. Old magazines can be a source of period material.

BOOKS

Many artists who are successful in the greeting card business swear by children's books for their primary inspiration. This is consistent with the kind of light touch, positive outlook, and emotional, fun quality of innocence that often typifies the successful greeting card. Frequently there is a distinctly childlike quality that characterizes these pieces.

MUSEUMS

If you are fortunate to live, work, or play in an area with even one good museum, by all means take advantage of it, if you're not already doing so. Learn all you can from accomplished artists. Seeing work firsthand is the best way. If that's absolutely impossible because of your locale, head for the books and study the masters. It's all there for you: color, composition, style, and spirit!

SPECIFIC SUBJECT
MATTER

If your specialty is flowers, grow some! Or buy some real ones. Work from real life or any actual subject matter whenever you can. This can be cumbersome or expensive. But if it's possible, it's well worth it.

CATALOGS

You call all that stuff in your mailbox junk? It's gold. If you order just one or two things through the mail, you will soon find yourself on every mailing list known to humanity. Like the colors on a page? Rip it out and put it in your color file. You now have a great palette for your next card. Need photos of children for a Juvenile idea? Order one or two Baby or Birthday gifts for kids through the mail and soon you'll be receiving catalogs crammed full of free photos of kids in great poses wearing fun clothes and surrounded by terrific kiddie props. A word of warning: These photos are the creative work of a photographer and as such are copyrighted, so use this material for anatomy or subject matter references. Never copy an entire photograph as an illustrated piece.

Gardening catalogs are wonderful for Floral research (the same warning applies here as it does to photographs). Upscale women's clothing keeps you attuned to the trendy. Sporting goods catalogs provide great Masculine research: tie patterns, shirt patterns, colors, topics, settings, decoys, and so on.

GREETING CARDS

Finally, however, in addition to conducting your research, you *must* keep abreast of what's going on in greeting cards. Get into those card shops! Then get out there again! Go at least once during each different season of the year. The product mix will change as various seasonal displays change within the stores. Study your competition (if you're selling professionally) and the state of the art (if you're just puttering around for fun).

PERSONAL PERSPECTIVE
Don Macken

"As a general business major in college it never dawned on me that anything to do with art or greeting card design was in my future. So I took the polar route to becoming Executive Vice President and Creative Director of Lasercraft.

Shortly after graduation in 1968 my brother, John, and I started a company, Optical Engineering, in his garage where we manufactured scientific equipment. Since the devices were used with lasers, we had one (which John designed and built) for testing purposes. As a hobby we would sometimes experiment by using the laser to carve images into wood. The eventual result was a second company: Lasercraft. Currently employing 130, Lasercraft sells products primarily in the giftware and specialty advertising markets. Until recently virtually all these products were made of wood with laser engraved images.

A few years back John came up with two patents on how to laser-cut paper. The company eventually constructed a 10,000-watt, sheet-fed laser system. It was this technology that prompted our growth into the stationery and greeting card markets. Although Special Friends, our primary card line at present, features laser-cut accents, we are told that it's the illustration style and specific designs that attract purchasers. The majority of the current line is illustrated from photographs that I've planned and taken. I have no formal design or art training. I've learned how to compose through a viewfinder, the importance of using a tripod, and that basic 35mm photography is not difficult. Most of what I know comes from intuition, extensive reading, and the creativity that is all around us at Lasercraft.

Special Friends' primary inspiration springs from my relationship with my wife and our three children. Because of them, I am continually allowed access to a very special, very delightful world. There is a short jump between the things the children invent as games and the things I make as card designs. Their toys are constantly used as reference material. Many of the Special Friends designs begin with photos that I take at home in the living room or on the deck. Having the children buzzing around, looking through the viewfinder, making suggestions is one of the ways I leave myself open to spontaneity.

The children have exposed me to over 500 illustrated story books from the library. The special look of Special Friends was heavily influenced by the illustrations that I admired in the very best of these books.

Another major influence is the book *How I Make a Picture* by Norman Rockwell (Watson-Guptill Publications, New York). This is a collection of his lecture notes from the art classes he taught in his later years, which the publisher has combined with various illustrations, sketches, and original photo references. In it Rockwell critiques his own work, explaining how he got his ideas, and showing you each of the behind-the-scenes steps he took to create his cover illustrations. Take my word for it. If you're interested in creating card designs that capture emotion and accurate physical detail, this book is for you.

The Rockwell book also helped me understand the timesaving and creative potential of projection devices. I currently have inexpensive Artographs in both my office and home studio. We have three others that we loan to our freelance illustrators from time to time.

The personality and style of Special Friends took us about four months to create. It was mainly a process of combining already-existing, but somewhat unrelated, influences with an awareness of what is currently working in the marketplace. If you do it right, you come up with something that is perceived as new and different.

When I read somewhere that a certain greeting card artist could create three, six, ten, or "on a good day, *twenty*" new card designs, I fell out of my chair. As I build a structure for each card, my goal is five a week. But due to other responsibilities, my current average is two or three. The process of putting together a structure for each card is hardly the same twice in a row.

Always keeping an eye out for unique situations, settings, and props in my everyday environment has led to the creation of some great designs. I've found that a liberal attitude toward photography is also necessary. It doesn't take much inspiration for me to decide to shoot a picture. However, usually I'll invest the time to carefully compose even a straight reference shot, because often that's all it'll take to get me far enough into it to dream up the missing ingredient necessary to turn a scene into a story. Although I may have a general concept of what I want, it isn't until I start working with the camera that the design really starts to gel. If I'm disappointed after the prints are developed, but still believe in the idea, I'll reconstruct the set or situation and shoot it over.

The photography equipment I use is of good quality—a Nikon FE2 with a motor drive which lets me shoot multiple frames continuously without having to advance the film by hand; a Sigma 50–200 zoom lens which gives me the flexibility of framing my subject tighter or looser without having to physically change position; and a Bogen floating-head video tripod. I shoot mostly print film so I can easily enlarge or reduce the prints on my Artograph projector.

A lot of decision-making and ad-libbing goes on during the sketch phase of the conceptualizing process. Although the pictures contain all the basic information, often I'll add small elements or perhaps reposition or even eliminate some at this stage. When I'm doing a rough mockup, I'm often composing from more than one photograph, rising to the challenge of relative scale and so on. For example, I may take a child's body position from one shot, head position from another, and props from a third. As I'm developing this sketch, I keep careful notes of exactly how I'm departing from each photograph for the illustrator who will ultimately do the finished artwork. Suggestions for changes, like lighting, for example, are also noted at this point. Once complete, the rough mockup and accompanying notes contain all the information the illustrator needs. We then sit down with the illustrator and review the mockup, notes, and photos. The basics of the composition are lightly pencilled in following the mockup and detail is added from the photo references. At long last the actual illustration has begun. Most Special Friends illustrations are done in watercolor, but some designs also include extensive amounts of linework, colored pencil, and gouache.

Once any finished illustration comes back to Lasercraft, there are still a tremendous number of design and production decisions that have to be made. We do this as a three-person team. It's important to have people whose opinions you trust and whose expertise you can count on to help you take it in for the touchdown.

In the step-by-step demonstration that follows you'll see the development of a card from the Special Friends line."

1. *The idea for this card originated when my family was camping in the Sierras. I found a picturesque creek setting and started photographing it. Then I had Anna, aged five, pose beside the creek. At first I had her reach out for something, which I intended to choose later when working up the final illustration. But the reflective pose you see here was so inspiring I chose it instead.*

2. *This rough color sketch was the next phase in the conceptualization process. Any changes from the photograph are noted at this stage for the illustrator.*

3. *The final watercolor reflects peaceful beauty and sensitive imagination, which work well with the inside editorial.*

4. *My secretary, Linda, loved the final illustration and came up with the sentiment, "dare to dream," which later became "take time to dream."*

take time to dream ...

Silvery moons & shooting stars
Are fine and fair to see, but
Friends like you, steadfast & true,
Mean so much more to me.

10
WRITING THE GREETING

Now, more than ever before, artists, illustrators, and designers are writing their own editorial for the greeting cards they create. You too can write for your own greeting cards if you just keep a few basics in mind.

Take another look at Chapters 1 and 4 with writing as your focus. The sending situation is the first and foremost issue when writing your greeting card. You *must* know what sending situation you want your card to be right for and what you want that card to accomplish for it to be successful. Once you have determined your sending situation, then you must determine the style in which your card will be written. Keep in mind the look of your card when you're making your choice. Determine which writing style will most appeal to the person to whom the card's visual style will appeal.

VERSE

Verse can be easy or it can be difficult. Which it is depends on your attitude about it. If you begin by believing that you *cannot* do it, then you definitely will not be able to. But if you just relax about it and believe

that you *might* be able to, then you've got a really good chance of succeeding. An excellent tool for writing verse is a rhyming dictionary. You can find one at your local bookstore (or order one if they're not in stock). Your local library is also an excellent source not only for this particular tool, but for many different kinds of books about writing in general, if you want to get into this in greater depth. Check at the reference desk; they'll be happy to help you out.

Remember to relax! Have fun with this! Sit somewhere in a comfortable chair and let your mind wander. As words and phrases capture your imagination or attention, jot them down. For example, if you're doing a Friendship card, perhaps the phrase "a friend like you" comes to mind. Look up "you" in the rhyming dictionary (or play around in your head if you're forgoing this tool) and pull out a few rhyming words that feel right. There's not really any right or wrong here (that's why you *can* do this); there's only what works for you and what doesn't. For example, you may come up with words like "blue," "do," and "true." The phrase "so true" comes. Play with that for awhile. Write ideas down as you go so you

This excellent example of verse on this Blank Card is beautifully illustrated in a manner totally in keeping with the delicacy of the poetry.

won't lose any. Listen to the meter or the beat (rhythm, time, tempo) of the words. Give each syllable a single beat. Perhaps you write:

> It's very true
> that I'm happy with
> a friend like you.

Change "It's very true" to "da-da-da-da" and "that I'm happy with" to "da-da-da-da-da" and finally "a friend like you" to "da-da-da-da." This shows you the meter is all right, but the poem lacks something.

Now try to do *more* with it. Try making it a compliment or make it warmer, more graceful, or sweeter.

> Nothing else
> could be so true,
> What a joy. . . .
> a friend like you!

An excellent example of this kind of verse or poetry appropriate for a Romantic Love situation is:

> You're the one
> I want to share my life with,
> Who makes our love
> a lovely place to be . . .
> You're the one
> who makes my world so perfect—
> for you're the one
> who means the world
> to me

> © RICHIE TANKERSLEY CUSICK

The illustration of the couple, shown on page 140, is a wonderful example of verse and artwork, working perfectly together.

It's not essential for all verse or poetry to rhyme. Sometimes the meter alone or a certain rhythm is enough when combined with beautiful imagery to create a poem. For example:

> With you
> there is sunshine
> the music of laughter
> warm moments to cherish
> sweet dreams to come true . . .
> With you
> There's tomorrow
> and bright new beginnings
> such happy forevers—
> with you and your love.

> © RICHIE TANKERSLEY CUSICK

The illustration shown right is a good example of poetry and artwork perfectly blended with one another.

"I love you, Dad"

What can you say
to someone who has
always been one of
the most essential parts of your world,
someone who took you by the hand
  when you were little
and helped to show the way...

What do you say to someone
who stood by to help you grow,
providing love, strength and support
so you could become the person
  you are today?

What can you say to let him know
that he's the best there is,
and that you hope you've inherited
  some of his wisdom and his strength?

What words would you say
  if you ever got the chance?

Maybe you just say
  "I love you, Dad..."

and hope he understands.

~Andrew Tawney

Poetry need not rhyme to be effective, as is most aptly illustrated here. There is no inside editorial.

"I have always loved writing. As far back as I can remember, I was always writing something, whether it was a story, a poem, or a song. And I have always loved greeting cards—both sending them and receiving them! So maybe it was inevitable that I should become a writer in the social expression industry. I began working for a major Midwestern greeting card company more than 11 years ago.

In all my years of experience, I've been approached by many people expressing a desire to write greeting cards because "they seem so easy to write." Nothing could be further from the truth! A greeting card, when done well, is deceptively simple. In actuality it requires talent, a love for words, and hard work to master this craft.

It's not always easy organizing the feelings you'd like to express to someone, the things you'd like the person to know. In conversational prose, where the mood is more casual, it's often permissable to use a more direct approach, such as "You're the greatest!" But for longer types of writing, prose or poetry, rhymed or unrhymed, there is the problem of crowding message and mood into a given number of words or lines. I use several techniques to help me.

I keep word cards handy, ready to refer to at a moment's notice. I keep them for every season, for example, Christmas, Valentine's Day, Halloween; for everyday occasions, Birthday, Anniversary, Sympathy; and also for more general categories such as Love, Children, Friendship. Let's take Thanksgiving, for example. On my Thanksgiving word card, I list all the words I can think of that conjure up images of Thanksgiving. I've always felt that images are extremely important in greeting cards. Whole moods can be set, feelings stirred, memories and dreams awakened by using just the right words. Keep in mind the five senses: Make the reader see, hear, feel, taste, and smell the Thanksgiving season. Consider words and phrases like "crisp, cold air," "turkey baking," "leaves crackling," "families gathered together," "laughing," "creamy pumpkin pie," "glowing." All these make up a warm, cozy image of a special Thanksgiving. I also include other words pertaining to harvest, autumn, countryside, thankfulness, prayer, and blessings.

The Everyday categories are handled much the same way. For example, on my Birthday word card, I collect words and phrases pertaining to parties, fun years, dreams, accomplishments, getting older. I list the positive aspects of aging, not the negative. Birthdays should not be regarded as occasions to regret the past, but as celebrations of achievements and new hopes for the future.

For your Sympathy word card, collect words pertaining to comfort, friends, understanding, being there, and sharing. Unless the card is specifically Religious, it's best to avoid references to God or an afterlife. Not all people share the same beliefs about death, and this can severely limit your audience. Be careful also in mentioning words like "loss" or "grief"; don't dwell on them. I try to avoid these altogether or at least keep them to a minimum. People don't need to be reminded of what they've lost, but of what they still have—the love and concern of friends who care.

Another technique is to keep rhyme cards for easy reference. Make separate lists of the rhymes you use most: "ay," "aring," "ove," for example. Fill them with all the rhyming possibilities you can think of. "Love" is always difficult, so experiment. Besides "of" and "above," try different phrases: "memory of," "reminder of," "proud of." Come up with your own combinations. A good greeting card is one that can say the same old thing in a fresh new way.

Browse through magazines and newspapers. Always be on the lookout for a catchy new phrase. Clip articles that spark ideas and save them. I have files and files of folders for all the seasons and holidays chock full of articles, stories, poems, and photos. You'll find that your files will be invaluable to you. Because most greeting cards are published so far in advance, I'm usually writing Christmas cards in the middle of the summer when it's hard to forget the sweltering temperatures and concentrate on Santa Claus! At times like these, your files will help you get in the appropriate mood.

Listen to records. Study song lyrics. Make note of unique phrasing; then create your own. Use your thesaurus. Make lists of synonyms. Let yourself go. Be silly! Make up nonsensical sound words for children's cards—"bumpety-bump" "tickly prickly"—fun things to make them laugh. Read, read, read! Gather quotes that you particularly like; these can be elaborated on and used for sentiment ideas. Experiment with different types of verse; try new structures, new rhyme schemes. Study other greeting cards and see what's selling, what the latest trends are. Ideas are everywhere if you just look. Don't take anything for granted. I confess, I save *everything* for research. I'm a hopeless pack rat!

All these techniques will be useful. But perhaps the most important aspect to keep in mind when writing is the recipient of the card. There are two things that help me in this respect: when applicable, I keep in mind one specific person—a close friend or relative—who might receive the card. For example, when asked to do a Grandmother card, I think of my own grandmother, the things I'd like to tell her, the different ways I appreciate her. If I don't have a specific person in mind, then I put myself in the place of the recipient. For example, if I were a teacher, what would I enjoy hearing from a student that would make me happy?

If all this sounds like work, it *is*! But it's also a lot of fun, and the rewards are terrific. A greeting card writer is speaking for millions of other people who all have feelings to express and at the same time is pouring out her (or his) own feelings for all the world to share. I believe a greeting card helps all of us realize we're not alone. We all have hopes and dreams, we make mistakes, we need to love and be loved, we sometimes suffer and lose things and people who really matter, we long to reach out, to have friends and to be friends. Each and every one of us is important. It's the greeting card writer who makes us aware of each other and helps us keep in touch. And in the hectic pace of today's world, that's a significant contribution!"

PROSE

Formal prose is the kind of writing that is traditionally associated with greeting cards. This kind of writing communicates its message very effectively, but in such a manner that you know for certain that the words written on the card were written by one person and the card is sent by another. There is a distance or lessening of emotion or personalness in this kind of writing. It does have a *huge* history of success and continues to succeed today. It is entirely appropriate for the more traditional greeting card to read:

> Wishing you and yours
> the special joys
> of the holiday season.

> © RICHIE TANKERSLEY CUSICK

Casual prose is the new direction in greeting card writing today. This kind of writing resembles conversation or the kind of words the person sending the card would be likely to actually say. An example is:

Whenever I remember beautiful things, you're always the first to come to mind.

> © RICHIE TANKERSLEY CUSICK

This approach enjoys ever-increasing popularity. This may be because we've come a long way toward speaking directly and openly about things that our parent's generation would only allude to. Whatever the reason,

Casual or conversational prose is a most effective way of writing for greeting cards. Note in this example how effectively the Stylized design supports the editorial without limiting it in any way. There is no inside editorial.

this form is generally easier to write because it's so close to what one would actually say in a given situation. The illustration shown right contains a very good example of this style of writing. The illustration of the person hiding behind a door, shown opposite, is a terrific example of prose used in a Humorous context. Note the very different design elements used in each and how effectively they each work.

Whichever style you decide to adopt (and you really should *try* them all), remember to use positive and uplifting kinds of words. Be supportive and complimentary at all times. Try to use a short word when you have a choice and, at the same time, try to create something beautiful and graceful, something that sounds like your art looks.

When *you* try writing, give yourself a break. Try lots of things. Try over a period of time. If you tried on Monday and were *sure* that writing was not for you, take another run at it on Thursday. Then leave it for a month or so, and if you're still discouraged, come back and try again later still. Sometimes you'll find that something has been working in your head without you even knowing it. It may pop up and surprise you! Don't give up. Doing your own writing as well as designing can be very satisfying and creates a very cohesive wholeness in your work.

Casual prose is very effective when used to create a Humorous card, as you can see in this example.

Can't you see
that I'm dieting?

PERSONAL PERSPECTIVE
RENEE LOCKS

" I never set out to illustrate greeting cards. The very first cards I did were hung on my bathroom mirror or refrigerator door as a silent way of communicating nourishing messages to myself and my five children without their having to respond, defend, or even relate to their mother pushing words of wisdom on them. Then friends asked for copies and like Topsy my cards just grew and are still growing.

I self-published my first cards and still do those that are not considered commercially viable. I usually print 250 at a time, and if color is needed, I design them so that one or two colors will bring them alive. I handpaint each one as a meditation.

To expand the number of people my cards connect with I considered dealing with a publisher. I researched *Artist's Market* (Writer's Digest Books, Cincinnati) to find a publisher with integrity and high-quality reproduction.

Most of what we are fed talks down to us, as if we the public were just so much fluff with cash in our pockets. I find that degrading and disempowering. I operate from the notion that when you relate with people sensitively and with intelligence, they will rise to the occasion.

Through the sumi brush I express my love of and relationship with nature. To me, the lessons of Mother Nature are a necessary part of our

physical, mental, and spiritual well-being. I feel that even if for a moment we remember to see the sky, trees, flowers, and moon our connection with all living things will be recalled. In our hectic times, it can be healing to look at a single blade of grass or a single flower. Because of my work in a peace center, I know the importance of peace starting within each of us. I would like my little cards to help us to get in touch with that peace.

Before I do any artwork I try to center myself, to focus on what I am doing and my meaning. I may not have an image or a word but there is a feeling of what is being expressed and I know from experience that when I stay focused and trust the process, I get to witness the magic of seeing a feeling manifest. I have been painting most of my life and doing calligraphy for over ten years, daily refining and perfecting what I do. Though I improve daily, I also know that the work has reached a degree of proficiency that I must honor. I always ask myself why am I using my art in this form; is there a need for what is being said; is there a way to express what I am inspired to express in a way that will be understood and elegant? My focus is clarity; that is number one, with both image and word. The test is how much I am willing to stay focused. I try to give each piece my all at that moment. If I am not interested in what I am doing, why should I expect anyone else to be?

I am trying to put into logical words what really comes from intuition, from an understanding that has grown out of my years of exploring and experimenting, failing and succeeding. I am not a conceptual artist. I describe myself as a "mature groper": meaning I grope my way to solutions.

I am concerned with content, integrity of my art, ac-

curacy, meaning, and appropriateness of the words and image. Some words inspire me and the design flows from that, or I have seen a face that stays with me and I want to paint it. I paint from memory. Then the face says something or induces a feeling, and the words flow from that. In a way the card designs me as much as I design it. It's a dance.

For me wandering around with my art, exploring, trying something I haven't tried before is important, important for the new challenge, the new solution to be found, the element of surprise and magic. It's like taking the back road instead of using the freeway.

At times I write things in letters, poems, or my journals that I am moved to share. I keep them on hand and when it feels right I use them on a card. I also really listen when people speak and sometimes they say something that tickles me or moves me and I will make a note of it. There is a danger that the person speaking is unconsciously quoting someone else so I always ask where they got it. Sometimes when I'm reading there will be something that fascinates me and I will write it down. I always attribute the source when I am aware of it. Then I also write poetry and use parts of my poems. Whatever words I choose, I try to use with the awareness that words carry an energy with them that we are responsible for.

I have been told that it is the words that sell a card. I don't know. I feel it is the total piece. Can you separate what makes a song a success, the words or the music? It is a couple; you can't have one without the other. Since the words and images seem like couples that have to find each other, they are equally easy or difficult for me. Sometimes one or the other will sit around for awhile until the right partner hooks up with it.

I have taught calligraphy to young folks and to women of means seeking ways to express themselves. I have also worked at a women's shelter and did cards they could hang there. Out of these experiences, I have come to understand that there are certain feelings we humans, young and old, rich and poor, all share. I saw that many women have never received the messages we need about ourselves in order to feel our own self-worth and our own beauty at any age or to understand that each of us has things to contribute. So the women cards grew out of my answer to that need: a need for sharing intelligent, mature, chewable thoughts and images. I consider the women to be characters on a stage and I listen for what they are saying.

If I did not think *greetings* were important I would not waste my time on them. That greetings fit so nicely on cards and can be shared with so many for so little is what makes greeting cards important to me. I see them as mini-messages, vitamins for our eyes and our minds, more intimate than the phone because you can hold them in your hands and read them over and over. We all love to and need to communicate with each other. Greeting cards are a way humans can do that. "

Through the use of the sumi brush, Renee Locks expresses her love of and relationship with nature.

Each morning is like being reborn...

we get another chance
to be
the best
that we can be.

147

APPENDIX:
MEDIA AND TOOLS

The Art Deco angularity of this postcard is evident not only in the border elements but also in the unique and fun treatment of the dancing couple.

THERE are a wide variety of media and tools that provide a host of possibilities for illustrating greeting cards. Read this section to discover how to use these media in your own unique way and which tools will help you create the effects you want. If, for example, you haven't experimented before with pastels or felt tip markers, take the time to acquaint yourself with some of their possibilities. Think in terms of the opportunities a media offers as well as its limitations.

COLORED PENCILS

Colored pencils will work in a wide variety of stylings if you make minor changes in the ways you use them. Their greatest limitation is that you are pretty much confined to the colors manufactured. You can change the colors slightly by overlapping them, and the shades by using more or less pressure or more or fewer layers of pigment. The paper texture you use for colored pencil work affects the look of the finished piece.

FELT TIP MARKERS

There are a multitude of different kinds of felt markers on the market today. There are many kinds of points available (more coming all of the time) and the colors can be deep or soft and pastel. There are even waterbased colors—far more choices than ever before.

GOUACHE

Gouache is a kind of water based paint. It may be the single most popular medium employed in the creation of greeting card art.

Gouache has a number of advantages. It can be either opaque or translucent. Essentially it's opaque in its original form and even more so when white is added; it becomes translucent when thinned with water.

The color range is extensive and the colors themselves are often the kind of light, bright ones that are entirely appropriate for the uplifting and positive note characteristic of the successful greeting card.

LIQUID WATERCOLORS

Brilliant colors and a delicate transparency are both characteristic of liquid watercolors, sometimes called dyes. The result in using this medium is a delicate tissue-thin feel: an advantage when creating designs for feminine appeal.

PASTELS

Pastel crayons are very fragile once applied. The looks achieved are often very spontaneous and fresh. The texture of the paper used in conjunction with this medium has a powerful impact on the final look of the work, so you'll want to experiment with a variety of papers.

WAX/OIL CRAYONS

A medium that's fun to work with, wax/oil crayons are available in bright, clear colors. Many effects can be achieved through experimentation. These crayons are much less fragile than the pastels.

PAPER

Most of the demonstrations included in this book were finished on a medium-surface, 2-ply bristol paper.

Bristol paper is manufactured in a

variety of surfaces from a very slick, smooth finish to a very rough one. It's also made in a variety of weights from 1- to 5-ply. Rarely, but occasionally, it's even heavier. The relative merits of the paper will depend on the material(s) you're going to apply to it as well as on your own personal preferences.

The rougher the paper, the greater the tooth, or grittiness, of the surface and, in the case of some materials, the greater the paper's capacity for holding or taking the material(s) applied. Very smooth papers are also appropriate in certain situations, for example, where the successful rendering of a very delicate detail is important. In this situation, the less surface interference the better.

The weight of the paper is a matter of end use and personal preference. Look over all your options and try out a couple of different ones to find the one that's exactly right for your design.

Tracing paper is an invaluable aid when sketching ideas for greeting card designs. Finely toothed vellum tracing paper will give you good results. Use this paper to trace over and keep what you want from earlier roughs while, at the same time, changing those elements you no longer like.

If you do elect to use tracing paper for your sketches, it's easy to transfer your final sketch to bristol or whatever paper you'll use for your finish by using the graphite transfer method. Just turn your final sketch over and retrace it, line for line, on its back side.

Turn it over to its right side and position it where you want on the paper you'll use for your finish. Tape it lightly in place. Now draw over your linework again using a little pressure. The lead on the back of the tracing paper will transfer to the paper upon which you'll be doing your finish. This step is illustrated in the demonstration on pastels on pages 62–63.

Some tracing papers are also available with a blue grid printed on them. They can be useful where you need mechanically accurate vertical and horizontal guides: lettering, general layout, high-tech designs, designs using a lot of architectural detail, and so on.

MECHANICAL PENCILS

A good mechanical pencil is a must. A variety of leads are available from very hard to very soft. You will need to experiment to determine which degree of hardness is right for you. Try out a few and change around a little after you've worked with one for awhile. Sometimes as your skills progress your needs will change.

PENS

If you plan to work in ink, then take a look at the terrific variety of technical pens available today. The pens themselves vary as well as the point sizes. The latter are interchangeable within some styles.

The array of point sizes enables you to vary the weight of your line as you draw. These pens usually have a highly controlled ink flow that produces linework of consistent width, consistent ink flow, reliable opacity, and quick drying time. However, if you want linework with more personality or more calligraphic character, then crow quill or chisel-edged pens may be more appropriate. These require a good deal of practice and skill to master. There are also many, many types of markers available.

RULER

A good quality cork-backed metal or metal-edged ruler will prove useful. You will use this ruler as a measurer, a cutting guide, and an inking guide, where appropriate. The cork backing keeps the ruler from slipping at crucial times, and it raises the edge of the ruler so that when or if you use it as an inking guide the edge won't grab the wet ink and draw it under, smearing your beautiful straight line.

The metal allows you to use the ruler as a permanent cutting guide because it cannot be gradually chopped to pieces with your knife, thus rendering it useless as a straight edge.

BRUSHES

Experiment with fine watercolor brushes for work requiring detail. It may take you awhile to find the perfect brush (or brushes) for your needs, but it's very, very important to do so. Acquire a number of sizes and use them; then try others. Red sable is the best quality. As your skills increase, you will develop special needs for brushes that do certain things. This can be an expensive undertaking, but one well worth it once you've found brushes that are perfect for you.

KNEADED ERASER

Kneaded erasers are just what they sound like, erasers made of rubber or plastic that are flexible and can be shaped. They are excellent for picking up linework or lightening areas of drawings, as well as thorough erasing.

CROP MARKS AND BLEEDS

While neither a media nor a tool, using crop marks and bleeds are important techniques for you to know. Indicate crop marks at the outside corners of your design to indicate where it ends or should be cut. For example, if you're doing artwork on a piece of paper that you intend to cut into a greeting card to send to a friend, it's a good idea to use a piece of paper that's larger than your finished card will be. An inch or two more is all you need. As you progress with the design, mark the corners to remind yourself where you will eventually cut the card.

If there is color that will go to the edge of the card, it's a good idea to extend it beyond the edge you've marked so that you won't interrupt the natural flow of your linework, brushwork, or evenness of tone as you put in large, solid areas of color.

When you extend your artwork a little beyond the indicated edges, you are creating a bleed. Then if you make a small error in cutting your card, no bare spaces will show through. This same principle applies for commercial work. Most manufacturers require about a ⅛" to ¼" bleed for any element that goes right up to the edge of the card. This includes linework as well as painted color.